THIS IS YOUR **PASSBOOK®** FOR ...

CAR INSPECTOR

NATIONAL LEARNING CORPORATION®
passbooks.com

Copyright © 2018 by

National Learning Corporation

212 Michael Drive, Syosset, NY 11791
(516) 921-8888 • www.passbooks.com
E-mail: info@passbooks.com

PUBLISHED IN THE UNITED STATES OF AMERICA

PASSBOOK® SERIES

THE *PASSBOOK® SERIES* has been created to prepare applicants and candidates for the ultimate academic battlefield – the examination room.

At some time in our lives, each and every one of us may be required to take an examination – for validation, matriculation, admission, qualification, registration, certification, or licensure.

Based on the assumption that every applicant or candidate has met the basic formal educational standards, has taken the required number of courses, and read the necessary texts, the *PASSBOOK® SERIES* furnishes the one special preparation which may assure passing with confidence, instead of failing with insecurity. Examination questions – together with answers – are furnished as the basic vehicle for study so that the mysteries of the examination and its compounding difficulties may be eliminated or diminished by a sure method.

This book is meant to help you pass your examination provided that you qualify and are serious in your objective.

The entire field is reviewed through the huge store of content information which is succinctly presented through a provocative and challenging approach – the question-and-answer method.

A climate of success is established by furnishing the correct answers at the end of each test.

You soon learn to recognize types of questions, forms of questions, and patterns of questioning. You may even begin to anticipate expected outcomes.

You perceive that many questions are repeated or adapted so that you can gain acute insights, which may enable you to score many sure points.

You learn how to confront new questions, or types of questions, and to attack them confidently and work out the correct answers.

You note objectives and emphases, and recognize pitfalls and dangers, so that you may make positive educational adjustments.

Moreover, you are kept fully informed in relation to new concepts, methods, practices, and directions in the field.

You discover that you arre actually taking the examination all the time: you are preparing for the examination by "taking" an examination, not by reading extraneous and/or supererogatory textbooks.

In short, this PASSBOOK®, used directedly, should be an important factor in helping you to pass your test.

CAR INSPECTOR

DUTIES

Car Inspectors, under supervision, maintain, inspect, test, examine lubricate, troubleshoot and make repairs and adjustments on any part of the Transit Authority's multiple-unit subway cars and subway service cars in the car shops, terminals, yards and on the road, including subway car, body electrical, electronic, mechanical and pneumatic equipment, truck equipment, body and truck brake rigging, electrical and pneumatic brake equipment, subway car bodies and associated fixtures, air conditioning and heating equipment, and electrical and electronic control and motor equipment; they maintain and repair subway car washers and shop equipment; operate and maintain lifting and carrying equipment associated with the placement and removal of subway cars and subway car parts; keep records and prepare reports; and perform related work.

EXAMPLES OF TYPICAL TASKS

Inspects air compressors for worn parts; tests belts for proper tension, replaces worn belts and makes necessary adjustments; examines motor mounts; examines brushes and brush holders and replaces brushes when necessary; inspects, cleans and replaces worn car body parts; checks controllers, batteries, lights and panel boards for proper operation and defects.

SCOPE OF THE EXAMINATION

The test may include questions on: electrical, electronic, mechanical and pneumatic principles and devices; the installation, testing, maintenance and repair of such devices; reading and understanding electrical and mechanical manuals and drawings; safe work practices and procedures; and other related areas.

HOW TO TAKE A TEST

I. YOU MUST PASS AN EXAMINATION

A. *WHAT EVERY CANDIDATE SHOULD KNOW*

Examination applicants often ask us for help in preparing for the written test. What can I study in advance? What kinds of questions will be asked? How will the test be given? How will the papers be graded?

As an applicant for a civil service examination, you may be wondering about some of these things. Our purpose here is to suggest effective methods of advance study and to describe civil service examinations.

Your chances for success on this examination can be increased if you know how to prepare. Those "pre-examination jitters" can be reduced if you know what to expect. You can even experience an adventure in good citizenship if you know why civil service exams are given.

B. *WHY ARE CIVIL SERVICE EXAMINATIONS GIVEN?*

Civil service examinations are important to you in two ways. As a citizen, you want public jobs filled by employees who know how to do their work. As a job seeker, you want a fair chance to compete for that job on an equal footing with other candidates. The best-known means of accomplishing this two-fold goal is the competitive examination.

Exams are widely publicized throughout the nation. They may be administered for jobs in federal, state, city, municipal, town or village governments or agencies.

Any citizen may apply, with some limitations, such as the age or residence of applicants. Your experience and education may be reviewed to see whether you meet the requirements for the particular examination. When these requirements exist, they are reasonable and applied consistently to all applicants. Thus, a competitive examination may cause you some uneasiness now, but it is your privilege and safeguard.

C. *HOW ARE CIVIL SERVICE EXAMS DEVELOPED?*

Examinations are carefully written by trained technicians who are specialists in the field known as "psychological measurement," in consultation with recognized authorities in the field of work that the test will cover. These experts recommend the subject matter areas or skills to be tested; only those knowledges or skills important to your success on the job are included. The most reliable books and source materials available are used as references. Together, the experts and technicians judge the difficulty level of the questions.

Test technicians know how to phrase questions so that the problem is clearly stated. Their ethics do not permit "trick" or "catch" questions. Questions may have been tried out on sample groups, or subjected to statistical analysis, to determine their usefulness.

Written tests are often used in combination with performance tests, ratings of training and experience, and oral interviews. All of these measures combine to form the best-known means of finding the right person for the right job.

II. HOW TO PASS THE WRITTEN TEST

A. NATURE OF THE EXAMINATION

To prepare intelligently for civil service examinations, you should know how they differ from school examinations you have taken. In school you were assigned certain definite pages to read or subjects to cover. The examination questions were quite detailed and usually emphasized memory. Civil service exams, on the other hand, try to discover your present ability to perform the duties of a position, plus your potentiality to learn these duties. In other words, a civil service exam attempts to predict how successful you will be. Questions cover such a broad area that they cannot be as minute and detailed as school exam questions.

In the public service similar kinds of work, or positions, are grouped together in one "class." This process is known as *position-classification*. All the positions in a class are paid according to the salary range for that class. One class title covers all of these positions, and they are all tested by the same examination.

B. FOUR BASIC STEPS

1) Study the announcement

How, then, can you know what subjects to study? Our best answer is: "Learn as much as possible about the class of positions for which you've applied." The exam will test the knowledge, skills and abilities needed to do the work.

Your most valuable source of information about the position you want is the official exam announcement. This announcement lists the training and experience qualifications. Check these standards and apply only if you come reasonably close to meeting them.

The brief description of the position in the examination announcement offers some clues to the subjects which will be tested. Think about the job itself. Review the duties in your mind. Can you perform them, or are there some in which you are rusty? Fill in the blank spots in your preparation.

Many jurisdictions preview the written test in the exam announcement by including a section called "Knowledge and Abilities Required," "Scope of the Examination," or some similar heading. Here you will find out specifically what fields will be tested.

2) Review your own background

Once you learn in general what the position is all about, and what you need to know to do the work, ask yourself which subjects you already know fairly well and which need improvement. You may wonder whether to concentrate on improving your strong areas or on building some background in your fields of weakness. When the announcement has specified "some knowledge" or "considerable knowledge," or has used adjectives like "beginning principles of…" or "advanced … methods," you can get a clue as to the number and difficulty of questions to be asked in any given field. More questions, and hence broader coverage, would be included for those subjects which are more important in the work. Now weigh your strengths and weaknesses against the job requirements and prepare accordingly.

3) Determine the level of the position

Another way to tell how intensively you should prepare is to understand the level of the job for which you are applying. Is it the entering level? In other words, is this the position in which beginners in a field of work are hired? Or is it an intermediate or advanced level? Sometimes this is indicated by such words as "Junior" or "Senior" in the class title. Other jurisdictions use Roman numerals to designate the level – Clerk I, Clerk II, for example. The word "Supervisor" sometimes appears in the title. If the level is not indicated by the title, check the description of duties. Will you be working under very close supervision, or will you have responsibility for independent decisions in this work?

4) Choose appropriate study materials

Now that you know the subjects to be examined and the relative amount of each subject to be covered, you can choose suitable study materials. For beginning level jobs, or even advanced ones, if you have a pronounced weakness in some aspect of your training, read a modern, standard textbook in that field. Be sure it is up to date and has general coverage. Such books are normally available at your library, and the librarian will be glad to help you locate one. For entry-level positions, questions of appropriate difficulty are chosen – neither highly advanced questions, nor those too simple. Such questions require careful thought but not advanced training.

If the position for which you are applying is technical or advanced, you will read more advanced, specialized material. If you are already familiar with the basic principles of your field, elementary textbooks would waste your time. Concentrate on advanced textbooks and technical periodicals. Think through the concepts and review difficult problems in your field.

These are all general sources. You can get more ideas on your own initiative, following these leads. For example, training manuals and publications of the government agency which employs workers in your field can be useful, particularly for technical and professional positions. A letter or visit to the government department involved may result in more specific study suggestions, and certainly will provide you with a more definite idea of the exact nature of the position you are seeking.

III. KINDS OF TESTS

Tests are used for purposes other than measuring knowledge and ability to perform specified duties. For some positions, it is equally important to test ability to make adjustments to new situations or to profit from training. In others, basic mental abilities not dependent on information are essential. Questions which test these things may not appear as pertinent to the duties of the position as those which test for knowledge and information. Yet they are often highly important parts of a fair examination. For very general questions, it is almost impossible to help you direct your study efforts. What we can do is to point out some of the more common of these general abilities needed in public service positions and describe some typical questions.

1) General information

Broad, general information has been found useful for predicting job success in some kinds of work. This is tested in a variety of ways, from vocabulary lists to questions about current events. Basic background in some field of work, such as sociology or economics, may be sampled in a group of questions. Often these are principles which have become familiar to most persons through exposure rather than through formal training. It is difficult to advise you how to study for these questions; being alert to the world around you is our best suggestion.

2) Verbal ability

An example of an ability needed in many positions is verbal or language ability. Verbal ability is, in brief, the ability to use and understand words. Vocabulary and grammar tests are typical measures of this ability. Reading comprehension or paragraph interpretation questions are common in many kinds of civil service tests. You are given a paragraph of written material and asked to find its central meaning.

3) Numerical ability

Number skills can be tested by the familiar arithmetic problem, by checking paired lists of numbers to see which are alike and which are different, or by interpreting charts and graphs. In the latter test, a graph may be printed in the test booklet which you are asked to use as the basis for answering questions.

4) Observation

A popular test for law-enforcement positions is the observation test. A picture is shown to you for several minutes, then taken away. Questions about the picture test your ability to observe both details and larger elements.

5) Following directions

In many positions in the public service, the employee must be able to carry out written instructions dependably and accurately. You may be given a chart with several columns, each column listing a variety of information. The questions require you to carry out directions involving the information given in the chart.

6) Skills and aptitudes

Performance tests effectively measure some manual skills and aptitudes. When the skill is one in which you are trained, such as typing or shorthand, you can practice. These tests are often very much like those given in business school or high school courses. For many of the other skills and aptitudes, however, no short-time preparation can be made. Skills and abilities natural to you or that you have developed throughout your lifetime are being tested.

Many of the general questions just described provide all the data needed to answer the questions and ask you to use your reasoning ability to find the answers. Your best preparation for these tests, as well as for tests of facts and ideas, is to be at your physical and mental best. You, no doubt, have your own methods of getting into an exam-taking mood and keeping "in shape." The next section lists some ideas on this subject.

IV. KINDS OF QUESTIONS

Only rarely is the "essay" question, which you answer in narrative form, used in civil service tests. Civil service tests are usually of the short-answer type. Full instructions for answering these questions will be given to you at the examination. But in case this is your first experience with short-answer questions and separate answer sheets, here is what you need to know:

1) Multiple-choice Questions

Most popular of the short-answer questions is the "multiple choice" or "best answer" question. It can be used, for example, to test for factual knowledge, ability to solve problems or judgment in meeting situations found at work.

A multiple-choice question is normally one of three types—

- It can begin with an incomplete statement followed by several possible endings. You are to find the one ending which *best* completes the statement, although some of the others may not be entirely wrong.
- It can also be a complete statement in the form of a question which is answered by choosing one of the statements listed.
- It can be in the form of a problem – again you select the best answer.

Here is an example of a multiple-choice question with a discussion which should give you some clues as to the method for choosing the right answer:

When an employee has a complaint about his assignment, the action which will *best* help him overcome his difficulty is to
  A. discuss his difficulty with his coworkers
  B. take the problem to the head of the organization
  C. take the problem to the person who gave him the assignment
  D. say nothing to anyone about his complaint

In answering this question, you should study each of the choices to find which is best. Consider choice "A" – Certainly an employee may discuss his complaint with fellow employees, but no change or improvement can result, and the complaint remains unresolved. Choice "B" is a poor choice since the head of the organization probably does not know what assignment you have been given, and taking your problem to him is known as "going over the head" of the supervisor. The supervisor, or person who made the assignment, is the person who can clarify it or correct any injustice. Choice "C" is, therefore, correct. To say nothing, as in choice "D," is unwise. Supervisors have and interest in knowing the problems employees are facing, and the employee is seeking a solution to his problem.

2) True/False Questions

The "true/false" or "right/wrong" form of question is sometimes used. Here a complete statement is given. Your job is to decide whether the statement is right or wrong.

SAMPLE: A roaming cell-phone call to a nearby city costs less than a non-roaming call to a distant city.

This statement is wrong, or false, since roaming calls are more expensive.

This is not a complete list of all possible question forms, although most of the others are variations of these common types. You will always get complete directions for answering questions. Be sure you understand *how* to mark your answers – ask questions until you do.

V. RECORDING YOUR ANSWERS

Computer terminals are used more and more today for many different kinds of exams.

For an examination with very few applicants, you may be told to record your answers in the test booklet itself. Separate answer sheets are much more common. If this separate answer sheet is to be scored by machine – and this is often the case – it is highly important that you mark your answers correctly in order to get credit.

An electronic scoring machine is often used in civil service offices because of the speed with which papers can be scored. Machine-scored answer sheets must be marked with a pencil, which will be given to you. This pencil has a high graphite content which responds to the electronic scoring machine. As a matter of fact, stray dots may register as answers, so do not let your pencil rest on the answer sheet while you are pondering the correct answer. Also, if your pencil lead breaks or is otherwise defective, ask for another.

Since the answer sheet will be dropped in a slot in the scoring machine, be careful not to bend the corners or get the paper crumpled.

The answer sheet normally has five vertical columns of numbers, with 30 numbers to a column. These numbers correspond to the question numbers in your test booklet. After each number, going across the page are four or five pairs of dotted lines. These short dotted lines have small letters or numbers above them. The first two pairs may also have a "T" or "F" above the letters. This indicates that the first two pairs only are to be used if the questions are of the true-false type. If the questions are multiple choice, disregard the "T" and "F" and pay attention only to the small letters or numbers.

Answer your questions in the manner of the sample that follows:

32. The largest city in the United States is
      A. Washington, D.C.
      B. New York City
      C. Chicago
      D. Detroit
      E. San Francisco

1) Choose the answer you think is best. (New York City is the largest, so "B" is correct.)
2) Find the row of dotted lines numbered the same as the question you are answering. (Find row number 32)
3) Find the pair of dotted lines corresponding to the answer. (Find the pair of lines under the mark "B.")
4) Make a solid black mark between the dotted lines.

VI. BEFORE THE TEST

Common sense will help you find procedures to follow to get ready for an examination. Too many of us, however, overlook these sensible measures. Indeed, nervousness and fatigue have been found to be the most serious reasons why applicants fail to do their best on civil service tests. Here is a list of reminders:

- Begin your preparation early – Don't wait until the last minute to go scurrying around for books and materials or to find out what the position is all about.
- Prepare continuously – An hour a night for a week is better than an all-night cram session. This has been definitely established. What is more, a night a week for a month will return better dividends than crowding your study into a shorter period of time.
- Locate the place of the exam – You have been sent a notice telling you when and where to report for the examination. If the location is in a different town or otherwise unfamiliar to you, it would be well to inquire the best route and learn something about the building.
- Relax the night before the test – Allow your mind to rest. Do not study at all that night. Plan some mild recreation or diversion; then go to bed early and get a good night's sleep.
- Get up early enough to make a leisurely trip to the place for the test – This way unforeseen events, traffic snarls, unfamiliar buildings, etc. will not upset you.
- Dress comfortably – A written test is not a fashion show. You will be known by number and not by name, so wear something comfortable.
- Leave excess paraphernalia at home – Shopping bags and odd bundles will get in your way. You need bring only the items mentioned in the official notice you received; usually everything you need is provided. Do not bring reference books to the exam. They will only confuse those last minutes and be taken away from you when in the test room.
- Arrive somewhat ahead of time – If because of transportation schedules you must get there very early, bring a newspaper or magazine to take your mind off yourself while waiting.
- Locate the examination room – When you have found the proper room, you will be directed to the seat or part of the room where you will sit. Sometimes you are given a sheet of instructions to read while you are waiting. Do not fill out any forms until you are told to do so; just read them and be prepared.
- Relax and prepare to listen to the instructions
- If you have any physical problem that may keep you from doing your best, be sure to tell the test administrator. If you are sick or in poor health, you really cannot do your best on the exam. You can come back and take the test some other time.

VII. AT THE TEST

The day of the test is here and you have the test booklet in your hand. The temptation to get going is very strong. Caution! There is more to success than knowing the right answers. You must know how to identify your papers and understand variations in the type of short-answer question used in this particular examination. Follow these suggestions for maximum results from your efforts:

1) Cooperate with the monitor

The test administrator has a duty to create a situation in which you can be as much at ease as possible. He will give instructions, tell you when to begin, check to see that you are marking your answer sheet correctly, and so on. He is not there to guard you, although he will see that your competitors do not take unfair advantage. He wants to help you do your best.

2) Listen to all instructions

Don't jump the gun! Wait until you understand all directions. In most civil service tests you get more time than you need to answer the questions. So don't be in a hurry. Read each word of instructions until you clearly understand the meaning. Study the examples, listen to all announcements and follow directions. Ask questions if you do not understand what to do.

3) Identify your papers

Civil service exams are usually identified by number only. You will be assigned a number; you must not put your name on your test papers. Be sure to copy your number correctly. Since more than one exam may be given, copy your exact examination title.

4) Plan your time

Unless you are told that a test is a "speed" or "rate of work" test, speed itself is usually not important. Time enough to answer all the questions will be provided, but this does not mean that you have all day. An overall time limit has been set. Divide the total time (in minutes) by the number of questions to determine the approximate time you have for each question.

5) Do not linger over difficult questions

If you come across a difficult question, mark it with a paper clip (useful to have along) and come back to it when you have been through the booklet. One caution if you do this – be sure to skip a number on your answer sheet as well. Check often to be sure that you have not lost your place and that you are marking in the row numbered the same as the question you are answering.

6) Read the questions

Be sure you know what the question asks! Many capable people are unsuccessful because they failed to *read* the questions correctly.

7) Answer all questions

Unless you have been instructed that a penalty will be deducted for incorrect answers, it is better to guess than to omit a question.

8) Speed tests

It is often better NOT to guess on speed tests. It has been found that on timed tests people are tempted to spend the last few seconds before time is called in marking answers at random – without even reading them – in the hope of picking up a few extra points. To discourage this practice, the instructions may warn you that your score will be "corrected" for guessing. That is, a penalty will be applied. The incorrect answers will be deducted from the correct ones, or some other penalty formula will be used.

9) Review your answers

If you finish before time is called, go back to the questions you guessed or omitted to give them further thought. Review other answers if you have time.

10) Return your test materials

If you are ready to leave before others have finished or time is called, take ALL your materials to the monitor and leave quietly. Never take any test material with you. The monitor can discover whose papers are not complete, and taking a test booklet may be grounds for disqualification.

VIII. EXAMINATION TECHNIQUES

1) Read the general instructions carefully. These are usually printed on the first page of the exam booklet. As a rule, these instructions refer to the timing of the examination; the fact that you should not start work until the signal and must stop work at a signal, etc. If there are any *special* instructions, such as a choice of questions to be answered, make sure that you note this instruction carefully.

2) When you are ready to start work on the examination, that is as soon as the signal has been given, read the instructions to each question booklet, underline any key words or phrases, such as *least, best, outline, describe* and the like. In this way you will tend to answer as requested rather than discover on reviewing your paper that you *listed without describing*, that you selected the *worst* choice rather than the *best* choice, etc.

3) If the examination is of the objective or multiple-choice type – that is, each question will also give a series of possible answers: A, B, C or D, and you are called upon to select the best answer and write the letter next to that answer on your answer paper – it is advisable to start answering each question in turn. There may be anywhere from 50 to 100 such questions in the three or four hours allotted and you can see how much time would be taken if you read through all the questions before beginning to answer any. Furthermore, if you come across a question or group of questions which you know would be difficult to answer, it would undoubtedly affect your handling of all the other questions.

4) If the examination is of the essay type and contains but a few questions, it is a moot point as to whether you should read all the questions before starting to answer any one. Of course, if you are given a choice – say five out of seven and the like – then it is essential to read all the questions so you can eliminate the two that are most difficult. If, however, you are asked to answer all the questions, there may be danger in trying to answer the easiest one first because you may find that you will spend too much time on it. The best technique is to answer the first question, then proceed to the second, etc.

5) Time your answers. Before the exam begins, write down the time it started, then add the time allowed for the examination and write down the time it must be completed, then divide the time available somewhat as follows:

- If 3-1/2 hours are allowed, that would be 210 minutes. If you have 80 objective-type questions, that would be an average of 2-1/2 minutes per question. Allow yourself no more than 2 minutes per question, or a total of 160 minutes, which will permit about 50 minutes to review.
- If for the time allotment of 210 minutes there are 7 essay questions to answer, that would average about 30 minutes a question. Give yourself only 25 minutes per question so that you have about 35 minutes to review.

6) The most important instruction is to *read each question* and make sure you know what is wanted. The second most important instruction is to *time yourself properly* so that you answer every question. The third most important instruction is to *answer every question*. Guess if you have to but include something for each question. Remember that you will receive no credit for a blank and will probably receive some credit if you write something in answer to an essay question. If you guess a letter – say "B" for a multiple-choice question – you may have guessed right. If you leave a blank as an answer to a multiple-choice question, the examiners may respect your feelings but it will not add a point to your score. Some exams may penalize you for wrong answers, so in such cases *only*, you may not want to guess unless you have some basis for your answer.

7) Suggestions
   a. Objective-type questions
      1. Examine the question booklet for proper sequence of pages and questions
      2. Read all instructions carefully
      3. Skip any question which seems too difficult; return to it after all other questions have been answered
      4. Apportion your time properly; do not spend too much time on any single question or group of questions
      5. Note and underline key words – *all, most, fewest, least, best, worst, same, opposite*, etc.
      6. Pay particular attention to negatives
      7. Note unusual option, e.g., unduly long, short, complex, different or similar in content to the body of the question
      8. Observe the use of "hedging" words – *probably, may, most likely*, etc.
      9. Make sure that your answer is put next to the same number as the question
      10. Do not second-guess unless you have good reason to believe the second answer is definitely more correct
      11. Cross out original answer if you decide another answer is more accurate; do not erase until you are ready to hand your paper in
      12. Answer all questions; guess unless instructed otherwise
      13. Leave time for review

   b. Essay questions
      1. Read each question carefully
      2. Determine exactly what is wanted. Underline key words or phrases.
      3. Decide on outline or paragraph answer

4. Include many different points and elements unless asked to develop any one or two points or elements
5. Show impartiality by giving pros and cons unless directed to select one side only
6. Make and write down any assumptions you find necessary to answer the questions
7. Watch your English, grammar, punctuation and choice of words
8. Time your answers; don't crowd material

8) Answering the essay question

Most essay questions can be answered by framing the specific response around several key words or ideas. Here are a few such key words or ideas:

M's: manpower, materials, methods, money, management
P's: purpose, program, policy, plan, procedure, practice, problems, pitfalls, personnel, public relations

    a. Six basic steps in handling problems:
      1. Preliminary plan and background development
      2. Collect information, data and facts
      3. Analyze and interpret information, data and facts
      4. Analyze and develop solutions as well as make recommendations
      5. Prepare report and sell recommendations
      6. Install recommendations and follow up effectiveness

    b. Pitfalls to avoid
      1. *Taking things for granted* – A statement of the situation does not necessarily imply that each of the elements is necessarily true; for example, a complaint may be invalid and biased so that all that can be taken for granted is that a complaint has been registered
      2. *Considering only one side of a situation* – Wherever possible, indicate several alternatives and then point out the reasons you selected the best one
      3. *Failing to indicate follow up* – Whenever your answer indicates action on your part, make certain that you will take proper follow-up action to see how successful your recommendations, procedures or actions turn out to be
      4. *Taking too long in answering any single question* – Remember to time your answers properly

IX. AFTER THE TEST

Scoring procedures differ in detail among civil service jurisdictions although the general principles are the same. Whether the papers are hand-scored or graded by machine we have described, they are nearly always graded by number. That is, the person who marks the paper knows only the number – never the name – of the applicant. Not until all the papers have been graded will they be matched with names. If other tests, such as training and experience or oral interview ratings have been given, scores will be combined. Different parts of the examination usually have different weights. For example, the written test might count 60 percent of the final grade, and a rating of training and experience 40 percent. In many jurisdictions, veterans will have a certain number of points added to their grades.

After the final grade has been determined, the names are placed in grade order and an eligible list is established. There are various methods for resolving ties between those who get the same final grade – probably the most common is to place first the name of the person whose application was received first. Job offers are made from the eligible list in the order the names appear on it. You will be notified of your grade and your rank as soon as all these computations have been made. This will be done as rapidly as possible.

People who are found to meet the requirements in the announcement are called "eligibles." Their names are put on a list of eligible candidates. An eligible's chances of getting a job depend on how high he stands on this list and how fast agencies are filling jobs from the list.

When a job is to be filled from a list of eligibles, the agency asks for the names of people on the list of eligibles for that job. When the civil service commission receives this request, it sends to the agency the names of the three people highest on this list. Or, if the job to be filled has specialized requirements, the office sends the agency the names of the top three persons who meet these requirements from the general list.

The appointing officer makes a choice from among the three people whose names were sent to him. If the selected person accepts the appointment, the names of the others are put back on the list to be considered for future openings.

That is the rule in hiring from all kinds of eligible lists, whether they are for typist, carpenter, chemist, or something else. For every vacancy, the appointing officer has his choice of any one of the top three eligibles on the list. This explains why the person whose name is on top of the list sometimes does not get an appointment when some of the persons lower on the list do. If the appointing officer chooses the second or third eligible, the No. 1 eligible does not get a job at once, but stays on the list until he is appointed or the list is terminated.

X. HOW TO PASS THE INTERVIEW TEST

The examination for which you applied requires an oral interview test. You have already taken the written test and you are now being called for the interview test – the final part of the formal examination.

You may think that it is not possible to prepare for an interview test and that there are no procedures to follow during an interview. Our purpose is to point out some things you can do in advance that will help you and some good rules to follow and pitfalls to avoid while you are being interviewed.

What is an interview supposed to test?

The written examination is designed to test the technical knowledge and competence of the candidate; the oral is designed to evaluate intangible qualities, not readily measured otherwise, and to establish a list showing the relative fitness of each candidate – as measured against his competitors – for the position sought. Scoring is not on the basis of "right" and "wrong," but on a sliding scale of values ranging from "not passable" to "outstanding." As a matter of fact, it is possible to achieve a relatively low score without a single "incorrect" answer because of evident weakness in the qualities being measured.

Occasionally, an examination may consist entirely of an oral test – either an individual or a group oral. In such cases, information is sought concerning the technical knowledges and abilities of the candidate, since there has been no written examination for this purpose. More commonly, however, an oral test is used to supplement a written examination.

Who conducts interviews?

The composition of oral boards varies among different jurisdictions. In nearly all, a representative of the personnel department serves as chairman. One of the members of the board may be a representative of the department in which the candidate would work. In some cases, "outside experts" are used, and, frequently, a businessman or some other representative of the general public is asked to serve. Labor and management or other special groups may be represented. The aim is to secure the services of experts in the appropriate field.

However the board is composed, it is a good idea (and not at all improper or unethical) to ascertain in advance of the interview who the members are and what groups they represent. When you are introduced to them, you will have some idea of their backgrounds and interests, and at least you will not stutter and stammer over their names.

What should be done before the interview?

While knowledge about the board members is useful and takes some of the surprise element out of the interview, there is other preparation which is more substantive. It *is* possible to prepare for an oral interview – in several ways:

1) Keep a copy of your application and review it carefully before the interview

This may be the only document before the oral board, and the starting point of the interview. Know what education and experience you have listed there, and the sequence and dates of all of it. Sometimes the board will ask you to review the highlights of your experience for them; you should not have to hem and haw doing it.

2) Study the class specification and the examination announcement

Usually, the oral board has one or both of these to guide them. The qualities, characteristics or knowledges required by the position sought are stated in these documents. They offer valuable clues as to the nature of the oral interview. For example, if the job involves supervisory responsibilities, the announcement will usually indicate that knowledge of modern supervisory methods and the qualifications of the candidate as a supervisor will be tested. If so, you can expect such questions, frequently in the form of a hypothetical situation which you are expected to solve. NEVER go into an oral without knowledge of the duties and responsibilities of the job you seek.

3) Think through each qualification required

Try to visualize the kind of questions you would ask if you were a board member. How well could you answer them? Try especially to appraise your own knowledge and background in each area, *measured against the job sought*, and identify any areas in which you are weak. Be critical and realistic – do not flatter yourself.

4) Do some general reading in areas in which you feel you may be weak

For example, if the job involves supervision and your past experience has NOT, some general reading in supervisory methods and practices, particularly in the field of human relations, might be useful. Do NOT study agency procedures or detailed manuals. The oral board will be testing your understanding and capacity, not your memory.

5) Get a good night's sleep and watch your general health and mental attitude

You will want a clear head at the interview. Take care of a cold or any other minor ailment, and of course, no hangovers.

What should be done on the day of the interview?

Now comes the day of the interview itself. Give yourself plenty of time to get there. Plan to arrive somewhat ahead of the scheduled time, particularly if your appointment is in the fore part of the day. If a previous candidate fails to appear, the board might be ready for you a bit early. By early afternoon an oral board is almost invariably behind schedule if there are many candidates, and you may have to wait. Take along a book or magazine to read, or your application to review, but leave any extraneous material in the waiting room when you go in for your interview. In any event, relax and compose yourself.

The matter of dress is important. The board is forming impressions about you – from your experience, your manners, your attitude, and your appearance. Give your personal appearance careful attention. Dress your best, but not your flashiest. Choose conservative, appropriate clothing, and be sure it is immaculate. This is a business interview, and your appearance should indicate that you regard it as such. Besides, being well groomed and properly dressed will help boost your confidence.

Sooner or later, someone will call your name and escort you into the interview room. *This is it.* From here on you are on your own. It is too late for any more preparation. But remember, you asked for this opportunity to prove your fitness, and you are here because your request was granted.

What happens when you go in?

The usual sequence of events will be as follows: The clerk (who is often the board stenographer) will introduce you to the chairman of the oral board, who will introduce you to the other members of the board. Acknowledge the introductions before you sit down. Do not be surprised if you find a microphone facing you or a stenotypist sitting by. Oral interviews are usually recorded in the event of an appeal or other review.

Usually the chairman of the board will open the interview by reviewing the highlights of your education and work experience from your application – primarily for the benefit of the other members of the board, as well as to get the material into the record. Do not interrupt or comment unless there is an error or significant misinterpretation; if that is the case, do not hesitate. But do not quibble about insignificant matters. Also, he will usually ask you some question about your education, experience or your present job – partly to get you to start talking and to establish the interviewing "rapport." He may start the actual questioning, or turn it over to one of the other members. Frequently, each member undertakes the questioning on a particular area, one in which he is perhaps most competent, so you can expect each member to participate in the examination. Because time is limited, you may also expect some rather abrupt switches in the direction the questioning takes, so do not be upset by it. Normally, a board member will not pursue a single line of questioning unless he discovers a particular strength or weakness.

After each member has participated, the chairman will usually ask whether any member has any further questions, then will ask you if you have anything you wish to add. Unless you are expecting this question, it may floor you. Worse, it may start you off on an extended, extemporaneous speech. The board is not usually seeking more information. The question is principally to offer you a last opportunity to present further qualifications or to indicate that you have nothing to add. So, if you feel that a significant qualification or characteristic has been overlooked, it is proper to point it out in a sentence or so. Do not compliment the board on the thoroughness of their examination – they have been sketchy, and you know it. If you wish, merely say, "No thank you, I have nothing further to add." This is a point where you can "talk yourself out" of a good impression or fail to present an important bit of information. Remember, *you close the interview yourself.*

The chairman will then say, "That is all, Mr. _____, thank you." Do not be startled; the interview is over, and quicker than you think. Thank him, gather your belongings and take your leave. Save your sigh of relief for the other side of the door.

How to put your best foot forward

Throughout this entire process, you may feel that the board individually and collectively is trying to pierce your defenses, seek out your hidden weaknesses and embarrass and confuse you. Actually, this is not true. They are obliged to make an appraisal of your qualifications for the job you are seeking, and they want to see you in your best light. Remember, they must interview all candidates and a non-cooperative candidate may become a failure in spite of their best efforts to bring out his qualifications. Here are 15 suggestions that will help you:

1) Be natural – Keep your attitude confident, not cocky

If you are not confident that you can do the job, do not expect the board to be. Do not apologize for your weaknesses, try to bring out your strong points. The board is interested in a positive, not negative, presentation. Cockiness will antagonize any board member and make him wonder if you are covering up a weakness by a false show of strength.

2) Get comfortable, but don't lounge or sprawl

Sit erectly but not stiffly. A careless posture may lead the board to conclude that you are careless in other things, or at least that you are not impressed by the importance of the occasion. Either conclusion is natural, even if incorrect. Do not fuss with your clothing, a pencil or an ashtray. Your hands may occasionally be useful to emphasize a point; do not let them become a point of distraction.

3) Do not wisecrack or make small talk

This is a serious situation, and your attitude should show that you consider it as such. Further, the time of the board is limited – they do not want to waste it, and neither should you.

4) Do not exaggerate your experience or abilities

In the first place, from information in the application or other interviews and sources, the board may know more about you than you think. Secondly, you probably will not get away with it. An experienced board is rather adept at spotting such a situation, so do not take the chance.

5) If you know a board member, do not make a point of it, yet do not hide it

Certainly you are not fooling him, and probably not the other members of the board. Do not try to take advantage of your acquaintanceship – it will probably do you little good.

6) Do not dominate the interview

Let the board do that. They will give you the clues – do not assume that you have to do all the talking. Realize that the board has a number of questions to ask you, and do not try to take up all the interview time by showing off your extensive knowledge of the answer to the first one.

7) Be attentive

You only have 20 minutes or so, and you should keep your attention at its sharpest throughout. When a member is addressing a problem or question to you, give him your undivided attention. Address your reply principally to him, but do not exclude the other board members.

8) Do not interrupt

A board member may be stating a problem for you to analyze. He will ask you a question when the time comes. Let him state the problem, and wait for the question.

9) Make sure you understand the question

Do not try to answer until you are sure what the question is. If it is not clear, restate it in your own words or ask the board member to clarify it for you. However, do not haggle about minor elements.

10) Reply promptly but not hastily

A common entry on oral board rating sheets is "candidate responded readily," or "candidate hesitated in replies." Respond as promptly and quickly as you can, but do not jump to a hasty, ill-considered answer.

11) Do not be peremptory in your answers

A brief answer is proper – but do not fire your answer back. That is a losing game from your point of view. The board member can probably ask questions much faster than you can answer them.

12) Do not try to create the answer you think the board member wants

He is interested in what kind of mind you have and how it works – not in playing games. Furthermore, he can usually spot this practice and will actually grade you down on it.

13) Do not switch sides in your reply merely to agree with a board member

Frequently, a member will take a contrary position merely to draw you out and to see if you are willing and able to defend your point of view. Do not start a debate, yet do not surrender a good position. If a position is worth taking, it is worth defending.

14) Do not be afraid to admit an error in judgment if you are shown to be wrong

The board knows that you are forced to reply without any opportunity for careful consideration. Your answer may be demonstrably wrong. If so, admit it and get on with the interview.

15) Do not dwell at length on your present job

The opening question may relate to your present assignment. Answer the question but do not go into an extended discussion. You are being examined for a *new* job, not your present one. As a matter of fact, try to phrase ALL your answers in terms of the job for which you are being examined.

Basis of Rating

Probably you will forget most of these "do's" and "don'ts" when you walk into the oral interview room. Even remembering them all will not ensure you a passing grade. Perhaps you did not have the qualifications in the first place. But remembering them will help you to put your best foot forward, without treading on the toes of the board members.

Rumor and popular opinion to the contrary notwithstanding, an oral board wants you to make the best appearance possible. They know you are under pressure – but they also want to see how you respond to it as a guide to what your reaction would be under the pressures of the job you seek. They will be influenced by the degree of poise you display, the personal traits you show and the manner in which you respond.

ABOUT THIS BOOK

This book contains tests divided into Examination Sections. Go through each test, answering every question in the margin. At the end of each test look at the answer key and check your answers. On the ones you got wrong, look at the right answer choice and learn. Do not fill in the answers first. Do not memorize the questions and answers, but understand the answer and principles involved. On your test, the questions will likely be different from the samples. Questions are changed and new ones added. If you understand these past questions you should have success with any changes that arise. Tests may consist of several types of questions. We have additional books on each subject should more study be advisable or necessary for you. Finally, the more you study, the better prepared you will be. This book is intended to be the last thing you study before you walk into the examination room. Prior study of relevant texts is also recommended. NLC publishes some of these in our Fundamental Series. Knowledge and good sense are important factors in passing your exam. Good luck also helps. So now study this Passbook, absorb the material contained within and take that knowledge into the examination. Then do your best to pass that exam.

———

EXAMINATION SECTION

EXAMINATION SECTION
TEST 1

DIRECTIONS: Each question or incomplete statement is followed by several suggested answers or completions. Select the one that BEST answers the question or completes the statement. *PRINT THE LETTER OF THE CORRECT ANSWER IN THE SPACE AT THE RIGHT.*

Questions 1-8.

DIRECTIONS: Questions 1 through 8, inclusive, are based on the paragraph *JACKS* shown below. When answering these questions, refer to this paragraph.

JACKS

When using a jack, a workman should cheek the capacity plate or other markings on the jack to make sure the device is heavy enough to support the load. Where there is no plate, capacity should be determined and painted on the side of the jack. The workman should see that jacks are well lubricated, but only at points where lubrication is specified, and should inspect them for broken teeth or faulty holding fixtures. A jack should never be thrown or dropped upon the floors such treatment may crack or distort the metal, thus causing the jack to break when a load is lifted. It is important that the floor or ground surface upon which the jack is placed be level and clean, and the safe limit of floor loading is not exceeded. If the surface is earth, the jack base should be set on heavy wood blocking, preferably hardwood, of sufficient size that the blocking will not turn over, shift, or sink. If the surface is not perfectly level, the jack may be set on blocking, which should be leveled by wedges securely placed so that they cannot be brushed or forced out of place. "Extenders" of wood or metal, intended to provide a higher rise where a jack cannot reach up to load or lift it high enough, should never be used. Instead, a larger jack should be obtained or higher blocking which is correspondingly wider and longer — should be placed under the jack. All lifts should be vertical with the jack correctly centered for the lift. The base of the jack should be on a perfectly level surface, and the jack head, with its hardwood shim, should bear against a perfectly level meeting surface.

1. To make sure the jack is heavy enough to support a certain load, the workman should   1.____

    A. lubricate the jack
    B. shim the jack
    C. check the capacity plate
    D. use a long handle

2. A jack should be lubricated   2.____

    A. after using
    C. only at specified points
    B. before painting
    D. to prevent slipping

3. The workman should inspect a jack for   3.____

    A. manufacturer's name
    C. paint peeling
    B. broken teeth
    D. broken wedges

4. Metal parts on a jack may crack if 4.____

    A. the jack is thrown on the floor
    B. the load is leveled
    C. blocking is used
    D. the handle is too short

5. It would NOT be a safe practice for a workman to 5.____

    A. center the jack under the load
    B. set the jack on a level surface
    C. use hardwood for blocking
    D. use *extenders* to reach up to the load

6. Wedges may safely be used to 6.____

    A. replace a broken tooth
    B. prevent the overloading of a jack
    C. level the blocking under a jack
    D. straighten distorted metal

7. Blocking should be 7.____

    A. made of a soft wood
    B. placed between the jack base and the earth surface
    C. well lubricated
    D. used to repair a broken tooth

8. A hardwood shim should be used 8.____

    A. between the head and its meeting surface
    B. under the jack
    C. as a filler
    D. to level a surface

9. When a long pipe is being carried, the front end should be held high and the rear end low. 9.____
The MAIN reason for this is to

    A. prevent injury to others when turning blind corners
    B. make it easier to carry
    C. prevent injury to the man carrying the pipe
    D. prevent damage to the pipe

10. As a serviceman, you notice a condition in the shop which you believe to be dangerous, but is under the jurisdiction of another department. 10.____
You should

    A. immediately notify your superior
    B. call the assistant general superintendent
    C. take no action, as your department is not involved
    D. send a letter to the department involved

11. All employees should regularly read the bulletin board at their job location MAINLY in order to   11._____

    A. learn what previously posted material has been removed
    B. show that they have an interest in the department
    C. see whether other employees have something for sale
    D. become familiar with new orders or procedures posted on it

12. The book of rules and regulations states that employees must give notice, in person or by telephone, at least one hour before they are scheduled to report for duty, of their intention to be absent from work.
The LOGICAL reason for having this rule is that   12._____

    A. the employees' time can be recorded in advance
    B. a substitute can be provided
    C. it allows time to check the employees' record
    D. it reduces absenteeism

13. When tools are found in poor condition, the reason is MOST often because of   13._____

    A. misuse of tools
    B. their use by more than one person
    C. defects in the manufacture of tools
    D. their use in construction work

14. When lifting a heavy object, a man should NOT   14._____

    A. twist his body while lifting
    B. bend knees
    C. have secure footing
    D. take a firm grip on the object

15. The MAIN purpose of the periodic inspection of machines and equipment is to   15._____

    A. locate stolen property
    B. make the workmen more familiar with the equipment
    C. discover minor faults before they develop into more serious conditions
    D. encourage the workmen to take better care of their equipment

16. If a serviceman does not understand a verbal order given him by his foreman, he should   16._____

    A. do the best he can
    B. ask for a different assignment
    C. ask the foreman to explain it
    D. look it up in the book of rules

17. A rule prohibits indulgence in intoxicating liquor, or being under its influence, while on duty. This rule is rigidly enforced in order to   17._____

    A. prevent an employee from endangering himself or others
    B. help reduce littering
    C. eliminate absenteeism
    D. help promote temperance

18. As a newly appointed serviceman, your foreman would expect you to 18.____

    A. make many blunders
    B. repair car equipment
    C. study car maintenance on your own time
    D. follow his instructions closely

19. Your work will probably be MOST appreciated by your superior if you 19.____

    A. continually ask questions about your work
    B. keep him informed whenever you think someone has violated a rule
    C. continually come to him with suggestions for improving the job
    D. do your share by completing assigned tasks properly and on time

20. One of your fellow workers has to leave work a half-hour early and asks you to punch his 20.____
time card for him.
You should

    A. punch out for him, but be sure to tell your supervisor
    B. tell him that no one is allowed to punch out someone else's time card
    C. punch out for him because you know he would do the same for you
    D. tell him he must promise to stay an extra half-hour tomorrow before you punch out
       for him

21. As far as is practicable, fiber rope should not be allowed to become wet, as this hastens 21.____
decay. The MOST logical conclusion to be drawn from this statement is that

    A. fiber rope is stronger than nylon rope
    B. shrinkage of wet rope is not a problem
    C. nylon rope is better than wire rope
    D. wet rope should be thoroughly dried before being stored away

22. The MAIN reason that gear cases are stacked on a pallet is to 22.____

    A. help servicemen find gear cases quickly
    B. help stockmen keep track of gear cases
    C. avoid hand-carrying of gear cases
    D. prevent damage to gear cases

23. If you are holding a heavy load by the pull rope on a block and tackle, your BEST proce- 23.____
dure is to

    A. let the rope hang loose
    B. snub the rope around a fixed object
    C. pull sideways to jam the rope in the block
    D. stand on the rope and hold the end

24. Modern electric power tools such as electric drills come with a third conductor in the 24.____
power cord, which is used to connect the case of the tool to a grounded part of the electric outlet.
The reason for this additional electrical conductor is to

A. protect the user of the tool should the motor short out to the case
B. provide for continued operation of the tool should the regular grounded line-wire open
C. eliminate sparking between the tool and the material being worked upon
D. provide a spare wire for additional controls

25. When a long ladder is being used, a length of rope should be tied from its lowest rung to a fixed support in order to prevent 25._____

    A. breaking the rungs
    B. the ladder from slipping
    C. anyone from removing the ladder
    D. anyone from walking under the ladder

26. When the level of the liquid in a storage battery on a Hi-lo truck is too low, the proper liquid to add to bring the level up to normal is 26._____

    A. salt   B. alkaline solution
    C. acid solution   D. distilled water

27. The MOST important reason for servicemen to keep their work areas neat and clean is that it 27._____

    A. makes more room for storage
    B. makes for happier workers
    C. prevents tools from being broken
    D. decreases the chances of accidents to workmen

28. The one of the following which is the BEST example of a material that does NOT burn easily is 28._____

    A. canvas   B. paper   C. wood   D. asbestos

29. The CHIEF reason for not letting oily rags or dust cloths accumulate in storage closets is that they 29._____

    A. look dirty
    B. may start a fire by spontaneous combustion
    C. take up space which may be used for more important purposes
    D. may drip oil onto the floor

30. The MOST logical reason for a serviceman to blow out electrical and mechanical equipment under car bodies before they are worked on by maintainers is to 30._____

    A. cool the equipment for the maintainers
    B. prevent rusting of equipment and parts
    C. prevent the maintainers from getting dirty while working
    D. prevent fires caused by heavy accumulation of dust

31. The liquid in heavy duty hydraulic jacks used in the car shops is 31._____

    A. water   B. oil   C. mercury   D. alcohol

32. It is not considered good practice to paint portable wooden ladders.   32.____
    The MOST logical reason for this is that the paint

    A.   would quickly wear off
    B.   might hide serious defects
    C.   might rub off on a supporting wall
    D.   would dry out the rungs

33. In order to lift a loaded pallet overhead by means of a crane, it would be MOST desirable   33.____
    to use a

    A.   single wire rope sling   B.   long crowbar
    C.   pallet sling   D.   rope splice

34. Of the following methods, the one which is the BEST way to keep rust off metal tools is to   34.____

    A.   keep them dry and oil them once in a while
    B.   air blast them
    C.   file or grind them often
    D.   wash them carefully with warm water

35. A Hi-Lo truck delivering a compressor to a work area approaches a closed door.   35.____
    The proper procedure for the Hi-Lo operator to follow is to

    A.   open the door while standing on the operating end of the Hi-Lo truck
    B.   open the door with the platform of the Hi-Lo truck
    C.   stop the Hi-Lo truck, wedge open the door, and then proceed
    D.   make a detour and follow a different path

36. The path between the two yellow lines on a main shop floor is used for   36.____

    A.   picking up and discharging workers that want a ride on a Hi-Lo
    B.   parking area for forklifts
    C.   the traffic path for Hi-Lo's and forklifts
    D.   storage of materials unloaded from Hi-Lo's

37. While on the way to a storeroom, you notice that oil has dripped on the floor from a jour-   37.____
    nal box and created a slipping hazard.
    You should

    A.   ignore it as it is not your doing
    B.   get some *speedi-dry* nearby and spread it over the oil
    C.   wait until you return from the storeroom to take care of it
    D.   call the supervisor and tell him about it

38. An employee always obeys the safety rules of his department because it has become a   38.____
    habit to work by these rules. This is

    A.   *good;* such a habit will get work done safely
    B.   *bad;* it is hard to change a habit
    C.   *good;* safety rules won't work if they have to be thought about
    D.   *bad;* safety rules should always be thought about before doing anything and not
         allowed to become a habit

39. If *you* are working in an inspection shop and you notice a trolley bug on one contact shoe of a car, it will mean that

39.____

    A. all contact shoes of the car are *live*
    B. only that contact shoe, that the bug is on, is *live*
    C. only the contact shoes, on the same side of the car that the bug is on, are *live*
    D. only the contact shoes of the one truck are *live*

40. It is necessary for a serviceman to wear a respirator when he is

40.____

    A. climbing a ladder
    B. operating a chipping gun
    C. blowing out the equipment under a car
    D. lubricating gear cases

_____

KEY (CORRECT ANSWERS)

1.	C	11.	D	21.	D	31.	B
2.	C	12.	B	22.	C	32.	B
3.	B	13.	A	23.	B	33.	C
4.	A	14.	A	24.	A	34.	A
5.	D	15.	C	25.	B	35.	C
6.	C	16.	C	26.	D	36.	C
7.	B	17.	A	27.	D	37.	B
8.	A	18.	D	28.	D	38.	A
9.	A	19.	D	29.	B	39.	A
10.	A	20.	B	30.	D	40.	C

_____

TEST 2

DIRECTIONS: Each question or incomplete statement is followed by several suggested answers or completions. Select the one that BEST answers the question or completes the statement. *PRINT THE LETTER OF THE CORRECT ANSWER IN THE SPACE AT THE RIGHT.*

1. The type of fire extinguisher which you would NOT use to extinguish a fire around electrical circuits is   1.__

    A. carbon dioxide   B. dry chemical
    C. water   D. dry sand

2. Artificial respiration is applied when an accident has caused   2.__

    A. breathing difficulties   B. loss of blood
    C. broken ribs   D. burns

3. Workers must NOT wear clothes that are too big when they work near moving machinery because   3.__

    A. that kind of dress will attract attention
    B. some part of the clothes can catch in the machinery
    C. big clothes get dirtier
    D. big clothes are hard to replace

4. The MOST likely reason why an employee should make out a report after using the contents of a first aid kit is that   4.__

    A. he will learn to write a good report
    B. unauthorized use may be prevented
    C. used material will be replaced
    D. a new seal may be provided

5. A shop employee is involved in an accident and severely injures his ankle. If a tourniquet were used, it would be to   5.__

    A. keep the ankle warm
    B. prevent infection
    C. prevent the ankle from moving
    D. stop the loss of blood

6. If a serviceman has frequent accidents, it is MOST likely that he is   6.__

    A. a man who works best by himself
    B. satisfied with his job
    C. violating too many safety rules
    D. simply one of those persons who is unlucky

7. In treating a cut finger, the FIRST action should be to   7.__

    A. wash it   B. bandage it
    C. request sick leave   D. apply antiseptic

8. When administering first aid to a person suffering from shock as a result of an accident, it is MOST important to   8._

A. keep him moving
B. prop him up in a sitting position
C. apply artificial respiration
D. cover the person and keep him warm

9. First aid instructions are given to some employees to 9.____

    A. eliminate the need for calling a doctor
    B. prepare them to give emergency aid
    C. collect blood for the blood bank
    D. reduce the number of accidents

10. The BEST reason for not using compressed air from an air hose for cleaning dust from 10.____
    clothing is that

    A. the clothing may be torn by the blast
    B. it is a dangerous practice
    C. this air contains too much moisture
    D. the air pressure will drop too low

11. Protective helmets give servicemen the MOST protection from 11.____

    A. falling objects   B. fire
    C. eye injuries   D. electric shock

12. Fuses are used in electric circuits 12.____

    A. so that electrical power tools cannot short circuit
    B. to burn out under an overload before electrical equipment is damaged
    C. to increase the amount of current that may be carried in the wires
    D. so that workmen can cut off the current without looking for the switch

13. The one of the following that is MOST effective in reducing the danger from hazardous 13.____
    vapors is

    A. immediate disposal of all wastes
    B. labeling all substances clearly
    C. maintaining good ventilation
    D. wearing proper clothing at all times

14. A serviceman should NEVER look into the arc from an electric welding torch. 14.____
    The BEST reason for this is that

    A. it can have a harmful effect on his eyes
    B. it will distract the welder from his work
    C. the serviceman is not allowed to operate a welding torch
    D. electric arc welding uses a large electrical current

15. The floors of 2 cars are to be painted with a special test paint. Assume that the floor area 15.___
    in each car is 600 square feet. A gallon of this paint will cover 400 square feet.
    The number of gallons of this paint that you should pick up at the storeroom to paint
    the 2 car floors would be

    A. 6   B. 5   C. 4   D. 3

16. Assume that you are sent to the storeroom for 1,000 of 600-volt contact tips which are to be distributed equally to 5 foremen, but you find that the storeroom can only supply you with 825.
If you distribute these 825 tips equally to the 5 foremen, the number of tips that each foreman will receive is   16.___

   A.   165   B.   175   C.   190   D.   200

17. You are asked to fill six 5-gallon cans of oil from a full drum containing 52 gallons. When you have filled the six cans, the number of gallons of oil left in the drun will be MOST NEARLY   17.___

   A.   14   B.   16   C.   22   D.   30

18. A certain wire rope is made up of 6 strands, each strand containing 19 wires.
The total number of wires in this wire rope is   18.___

   A.   25   B.   96   C.   114   D.   144

19. The hook should be the weakest part of any crane, hoist, or sling.
According to this statement, if a particular hook has a rated capacity of 21/2 tons, then the MAXIMUM load thatshould be lifted with this hook is _____ pounds.   19.___

   A.   150   B.   3,000   C.   5,000   D.   5,500

20. Assume that 2 car wheels weigh 635 pounds each and are attached to an axle weighing 1,260 pounds.
The total weight of this assembly is MOST NEARLY _____ pounds.   20.___

   A.   1,270   B.   1,520   C.   1,895   D.   2,530

21. If an employee authorizes his employer to deduct 4% of his $450 weekly salary for a savings bond, the MINIMUM number of weekly deductions required to get enough money to buy a bond costing $54 is   21.___

   A.   3   B.   6   C.   8   D.   9

22. In weighing out a truckful of scrap metal, the scale reads 21,496 lbs. If the empty truck weighs 9,879 lbs., the amount of scrap metal, in pounds, is MOST NEARLY   22.___

   A.   10,507   B.   10,602   C.   11,617   D.   12,617

23. Four trays of material are placed on the body of a delivery truck for delivery to the inspection shop. Each tray is 4 feet wide and 4 feet long.
If these trays are placed side by side on the floor of the delivery truck, together they will cover an area of the floor MOST NEARLY _____ square feet.   23.___

   A.   32   B.   48   C.   64   D.   72

24. Assume that you are operating a degreasing tank and its tray holds 5 gear cases. It takes 40 minutes to clean one tray of gear cases.
At the end of 6 hours of operation (excluding lunch break and loading and unloading time), the number of gear cases cleaned will be   24.___

   A.   30   B.   36   C.   45   D.   50

25. If a serviceman's weekly gross salary is $480, and 20% is deducted for taxes, his take-home pay is

    A. $360   B. $384   C. $420   D. $432

25._____

26. Two-thirds of 10 feet is MOST NEARLY

    A. 6'2"   B. 6'8"   C. 6'11"   D. 7'1"

26._____

27. You are directed to pick up a tray load of brake shoes.
The combined weight of tray and brake shoes is 4,000 pounds. Assume that each brake shoe weighs 40 pounds and the tray weighs 240 pounds.
The number of brake shoes in the tray is MOST NEARLY

    A. 88   B. 94   C. 100   D. 106

27._____

28. The one of the following materials that is used to protect equipment from rain is a

    A. sprinkler   B. tarpaulin
    C. compressor   D. templet

28._____

29. The use of wet rope near power lines and other electrical equipment is

    A. a dangerous practice
    B. sure to interrupt telephone service
    C. recommended as a safe practice
    D. common in the car shop but not in maintenance of way

29._____

Questions 30-34.

DIRECTIONS: Questions 30 through 34, inclusive, are based on the following paragraph, table, and floor plan. Each line in the table contains the name of a certain piece of car equipment together with its destination in the car shop. The floor plan shows a car shop divided into six areas, each with a different code number.

TABLE   CAR SHOP FLOOR PLAN

NAME OF CAR EQUIPMENT	DESTINATION IN CAR SHOP
Journal boxes	Degreasing tanks
Door operators	Car body shop Main
Air compressors	shipping Air brake shop
Unit valves	Truck shop Degreasing
Wheels Gear assemblies	tanks Main shipping
Unit switches Variable	Air brake shop
load units	
Motor couplings	Degreasing tanks
Motors Brake linkage	Truck shop Degreasing
Fan motors Batteries	tanks Car body shop
Motor generators	Main shipping Car body
	shop

Overhaul Shop	Air Brake Shop	Main Shipping
AREA 1	AREA 2	AREA 3

Degreasing Tanks	Truck Shop
AREA 4	AREA 5

Car Body Shop
AREA 6

In each of Questions 30 through 34, there are the names of four types of car equipment, and a code number for a destination in the car shop. In each question, select the CORRECT combination of equipment name and destination code number as determined by referring to the Table and Car Shop Floor Plan.

30.　A.　Motor generators: Area 6　　　　　　　　　　　　30.____
　　　B.　Fan motors: Area 5
　　　C.　Motor couplings: Area 1
　　　D.　Motor end housings: Area 2

31.　A.　Door operators: Area 3　　　　　　　　　　　　31.____
　　　B.　Air compressors: Area 5
　　　C.　Brake linkage: Area 4
　　　D.　Variable load units: Area 6

32.　A.　Batteries: Area 1　　　　　　　　　　　　　　32.____
　　　B.　Unit switches: Area 3
　　　C.　Motor controllers: Area 2
　　　D.　Fan motors: Area 4

33.　A.　Wheels: Area 2　　　　　　　　　　　　　　　33.____
　　　B.　Motor end housings: Area 6
　　　C.　Journal boxes: Area 3
　　　D.　Unit valves: Area 2

34.　A.　Gear assemblies: Area 4　　　　　　　　　　　34.____
　　　B.　Motor couplings: Area 3
　　　C.　Variable load units: Area 6
　　　D.　Unit valves: Area 5

35.　The drawing at the right is an assembly sketch.　　　35.____
　　　Study the sketch and select the CORRECT assembly
　　　procedure.
　　　A.　3 onto 4, 2 onto 5, 1 onto 5, and tighten
　　　B.　4 onto 3, 1 onto 5, 5 through 4 and 3, tighten 2
　　　　　onto 5
　　　C.　5 into 3, 2 and 1 onto 5, 4 into 3, and tighten
　　　D.　4 into 3, 5 through 3 and 4, 2 onto 5, 1 onto 5,
　　　　　and tighten

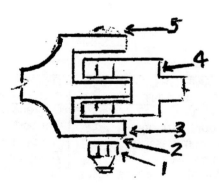

Questions 36-37.

DIRECTIONS:　Questions 36 and 37 are based on the following data and sketch. When
　　　　　　　answering these questions, refer to this material.

　　　The average clearance requirements for 2-ton, 3-ton, and 5-ton forklift trucks are shown
in the following sketch. Dimensions are: R, the overall length including loads S, the overall
widths T, the overall height; U, the minimum permissible width of aisle.

	2-Ton Truck	3-Ton Truck	5-Ton Truck
B	112	118	142
S	45	46	47
T	85	85	85
U	76	79	92

All dimensions are in inches.

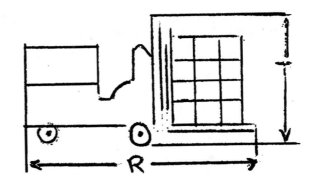

36. From the data given above, it can be seen that the overall length, including load, of a 3-ton truck is _____ inches.

    A. 85   B. 92   C. 118   D. 142

36._____

37. From the data given above, it can be seen that the overall height of a 2-ton truck is _____ inches.

    A. 47   B. 76   C. 79   D. 85

37._____

38.

38._____

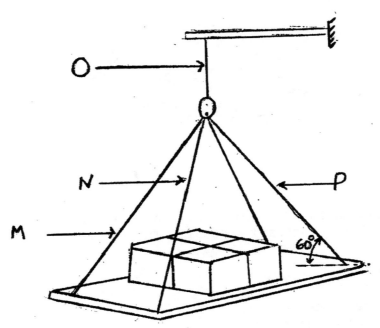

The above diagram shows a loaded sling suspended from a crane. The rope which carries the heaviest load is

    A. M   B. N   C. O   D. P

39. If the tray shown in the diagram at the right is being pushed in the direction shown by the arrows, it is MOST likely to move in the direction of the arrow shown in

39.____

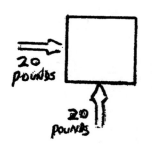

A.

B.

C.

D.

40.

40.____

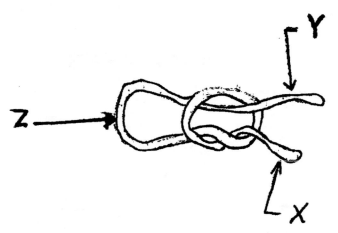

The above diagram shows a slip knot. The way this knot is nade, it would be CORRECT to say that the knot can be untied by pulling on line _____ while holding _____.

    A. X; line Z
    B. Y; line X
    C. X and line Y together; line Z
    D. Z; lines X and Y together

KEY (CORRECT ANSWERS)

1. C	11. A	21. A	31. C
2. A	12. B	22. C	32. B
3. B	13. C	23. C	33. D
4. C	14. A	24. C	34. A
5. D	15. D	25. B	35. D
6. C	16. A	26. B	36. C
7. A	17. C	27. B	37. D
8. D	18. C	28. B	38. C
9. B	19. C	29. A	39. B
10. B	20. D	30. A	40. B

EXAMINATION SECTION
TEST 1

DIRECTIONS: Each question or incomplete statement is followed by several suggested answers or completions. Select the one that *BEST* answers the question or completes the statement. *PRINT THE LETTER OF THE CORRECT ANSWER IN THE SPACE AT THE RIGHT.*

1. Asbestos was used as a wire covering mainly for protection against   1.____

    A. humidity   B. vibration   C. corrosion   D. heat

2. A wattmeter is used for making a direct measurement of   2.____

    A. current   B. voltage   C. power   D. resistance

3. The number of connection points to a two-pole, double-throw knife switch is   3.____

    A. 2   B. 4   C. 6   D. 8

4. Wires are pulled through conduit with the aid of   4.____

    A. a hickey   B. an extension bit
    C. a snake   D. a nipple

5. To smooth out the ripples present in rectified a.c., the device commonly used is a   5.____

    A. filter   B. relay   C. spark gap   D. booster

6. A tachometer is used for measuring   6.____

    A. r.p.m.   B. torque
    C. power factor   D. specific gravity

7. Rubber insulation deteriorates most rapidly when in contact with   7.____

    A. water   B. oil   C. lead   D. aluminum

8. The microfarad is a unit of measurement used for condenser   8.____

    A. ohmic resistance   B. power loss
    C. leakage current   D. capacity

9. A "megger" is an electrical instrument used to measure   9.____

    A. current   B. resistance
    C. voltage   D. wattage

10. When a run of conduit would require many right angle bends, it is necessary to install pull boxes because   10.____

    A. conduit cannot be bent
    B. otherwise injury to the wires may result during installation
    C. conduit comes in fixed lengths
    D. the conduit requires support

11. The metal frames of some electrical units are grounded mainly to   11.____

     A. eliminate short-circuits
     B. save insulating material
     C. protect against shock
     D. prevent overloading

12. A motor which can be operated only from an a.c. power source is   12.____

     A. a shunt motor   B. a series motor
     C. a compound motor   D. an induction motor

13. Of the following, the poorest conductor of electricity is   13.____

     A. mercury   B. sulphuric acid
     C. distilled water   D. salt water

14. The insulation provided between commutator bars on a d.c. motor is generally   14.____

     A. mica   B. lucite   C. porcelain   D. transite

15. Nichrome wire should be most suitable for use in   15.____

     A. a transformer   B. a motor
     C. an incandescent lamp   D. a heating element

16. Electrical outlet boxes do not have to be drilled for the entrance of conduit into the boxes if they are provided with   16.____

     A. bushings   B. knockouts   C. hickeys   D. couplings

17. The minimum number of field windings in a compound motor is   17.____

     A. 1   B. 2   C. 3   D. 4

18. The motor most likely to reach a dangerous speed if operated at normal voltage and no load is a   18.____

     A. shunt motor   B. series motor
     C. compound motor   D. synchronous motor

19. If three 6-volt batteries are connected in parallel, the resultant voltage will be   19.____

     A. 18 volts   B. 9 volts   C. 6 volts   D. 2 volts

20. If an incandescent lamp is operated at a voltage below its rated voltage then it   20.____

     A. will operate more efficiently
     B. will have a longer life
     C. will take more power
     D. is more likely to fail by arcing

21. Four resistors, having respective current ratings of 1, 2, 3 and 4 amperes, are connected in series. If the resistors are not to be overloaded, the maximum current permissable in this circuit is   21.____

     A. 1 ampere   B. 2.5 amperes
     C. 4 amperes   D. 10 amperes

22. Conduit is reamed mainly to   22.____

    A. protect the wires against sharp edges
    B. make threading easier
    C. increase its electrical conductivity
    D. improve its appearance

23. Two 25-watt, 120-volt lamps are connected in parallel to a 120-volt source. The two   23.____
    lamps will take a total of

    A. 12.5 watts   B. 25 watts
    C. 50 watts   D. 100 watts

24. An advantage of the mercury arc rectifiers when compared to rotary converters is that   24.____
    the mercury arc rectifiers

    A. are relatively quiet
    B. eliminate the use of transformers
    C. operate at lower voltage
    D. operate for shorter periods

25. A bushing is usually provided on the end of a conduit running into a panel box. An impor-   25.____
    tant function of the bushing is to

    A. insulate the conduit from the panel box
    B. support the panel box
    C. separate one conduit from another
    D. prevent injury to the wires

26. An alternator is   26.____

    A. an a.c. generator
    B. a ground detector device
    C. a choke coil
    D. a frequency meter

27. The best immediate first-aid treatment for a scraped knee is to   27.____

    A. apply plain vaseline
    B. use a knee splint
    C. apply heat
    D. wash it with soap and water

Questions 28 - 34.

Questions 28 through 34 are based on the Signal System Emergency Power Supply Information given below. Read this information carefully before answering these questions.

SIGNAL SYSTEM EMERGENCY POWER SUPPLY INFORMATION

The signal mains operate on 115 volts a.c. and are fed from either a normal power supply or an
emergency power supply. When the normal power supply goes below 90 volts, a transfer switch
automatically switches the signal mains to the emergency power. With normal feed, the transfer
switch is held in the normal or energized position. When the normal power supply falls, the
transfer switch changes to the emergency supply by means of gravity and a control spring. The

operation of the transfer switch is controlled by means of a potential relay which opens on less than 90 volts. Once the transfer switch has changed to the emergency side, it can only be reset to the normal side by first closing the potential relay by hand. If the normal supply is satisfactory, this relay will remain closed. Then by pushing a reset button, the transfer switch will swing to the normal side and remain-closed through its retaining circuit. A special push button is provided for checking the transfer switch for proper operation.

28. The transfer switch will automatically connect the signal mains to emergency power when the normal power supply voltage is   28.___

    A. 120 volts   B. 115 volts   C. 95 volts   D. 85 volts

29. The *FIRST* step in resetting the transfer switch to the normal side is to   29.___

    A. open the potential relay   B. push the reset button
    C. operate the special button   D. close the potential relay

30. The special push button is provided for   30.___

    A. checking the operation of the transfer switch
    B. disconnecting the emergency supply
    C. automatically closing the potential relay
    D. resetting the control spring

31. The reset button is used to   31.___

    A. swing the transfer switch to the normal side
    B. swing the transfer switch to the emergency side
    C. energize the potential relay
    D. de-energize the potential relay

32. The signal mains receive their power through the   32.___

    A. potential relay   B. transfer switch
    C. reset button   D. special push button

33. When the emergency power is feeding the signal mains, then the   33.___

    A. transfer switch is automatically energized
    B. potential relay automatically goes to the closed position
    C. transfer switch is in the de-energized position
    D. special push button must be pressed to restore the normal power supply

34. The transfer switch is held in the emergency supply position by   34.___

    A. a retaining circuit
    B. a special push button
    C. gravity and a control spring
    D. a reset button

35. To reduce the pitting of relay contacts which make and break frequently, the unit generally connected across them is a   35.___

    A. transistor   B. spark gap
    C. condenser   D. switch

36. As compared to a solid conductor, a stranded conductor of the same diameter 36._____

    A. has greater flexibility
    B. requires less insulation
    C. has greater resistance to corrosion
    D. does not require soldered connections

37. The electrolyte in a lead storage battery is 37._____

    A. sodium bicarbonate
    C. muriatic acid
    B. sulphuric acid
    D. ammonia

38. Twisted pair wire is desirable for telephone circuits mainly because it 38._____

    A. is less likely to pick up electrical interference
    B. can be run in long stretches without any support
    C. can carry heavy currents
    D. can withstand high voltage

39. In the subway, heavy copper bonds are connected across the joints of the track rails. With the bonds installed, a voltage drop measurement is taken across the track rail joint. This test would be used mainly to determine the bond 39._____

    A. temperature
    C. breakdown voltage
    B. electrical resistance
    D. leakage current

40. In a polarized electric cord plug, the contact blades of the plug are 40._____

    A. magnetized
    B. of different color
    C. parallel to each other
    D. perpendicular to each other

41. A capacity rating expressed in ampere-hours is commonly used for 41._____

    A. insulators
    C. switches
    B. storage batteries
    D. inductances

42. The number of ordinary flashlight cells which must be connected together to obtain 6 volts is 42._____

    A. 1   B. 2   C. 3   D. 4

43. A bank of five 120-volt lamps connected in series is used for test purposes in the subway. This test bank would be best utilized in checking a circuit having 43._____

    A. 120 volts d.c.
    C. 24 volts
    B. 120 volts a.c.
    D. 600 volts

44. A step-up transformer is used to step up 44._____

    A. voltage   B. current   C. power   D. frequency

45. A photoelectric cell is a device for changing   45.____

    A. light into electricity
    B. electricity into light
    C. electricity into heat
    D. sound into electricity

46. Decreasing the length of a wire conductor will   46.____

    A. increase the current carrying capacity
    B. decrease the current carrying capacity
    C. decrease the resistance
    D. increase the resistance

47. The proper tool to use in making a hole through a transite panel is   47.____

    A. a star drill   B. a countersink
    C. a twist drill   D. an auger

48. Copper is a preferred metal in the construction of large knife switches because it is   48.____

    A. soft   B. flexible
    C. a good conductor   D. light in weight

49. The process of removing the insulation from a wire is called   49.____

    A. sweating   B. skinning
    C. tinning   D. braiding

50. The electric lamp which is used for providing heat is   50.____

    A. a sodium vapor lamp   B. a mercury vapor lamp
    C. a neon lamp   D. an infra-red lamp

KEY (CORRECT ANSWERS)

1.	D	11.	C	21.	A	31.	A	41.	B
2.	C	12.	D	22.	A	32.	B	42.	D
3.	C	13.	C	23.	C	33.	C	43.	D
4.	C	14.	A	24.	A	34.	C	44.	A
5.	A	15.	D	25.	D	35.	C	45.	A
6.	A	16.	B	26.	A	36.	A	46.	C
7.	B	17.	B	27.	D	37.	B	47.	C
8.	D	18.	B	28.	D	38.	A	48.	C
9.	B	19.	C	29.	D	39.	B	49.	B
10.	B	20.	B	30.	A	40.	D	50.	D

TEST 2

DIRECTIONS: Each question or incomplete statement is followed by several suggested answers or completions. Select the one that *BEST* answers the question or completes the statement. *PRINT THE LETTER OF THE CORRECT ANSWER IN THE SPACE AT THE RIGHT.*

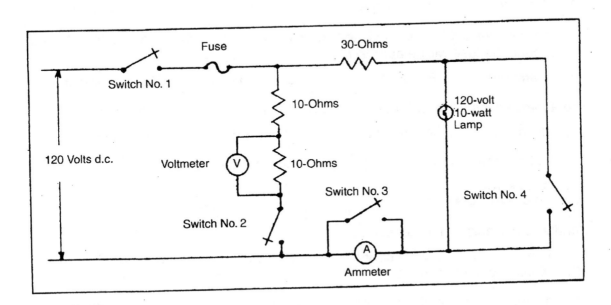

Questions 1-7

Questions 1 through 7 are based on the above wiring diagram. Refer to this diagram when answering these questions.

1. Starting with all switches open, then to light the lamp it is necessary to close switch   1._____

     A. No. 1   B. No. 2   C. No. 3   D. No . 4

2. Closing one of the four switches will prevent the lamp from being lighted. This switch is   2._____

     A. No. 1   B. No. 2   C. No. 3   D. No. 4

3. The two switches which must be in the closed position to obtain a reading on the voltme-   3._____
    ter are

     A. No. 1 and No. 4   B. No. 2 and No. 3
     C. No. 3 and No. 4   D. No.1 and No. 2

4. To obtain a reading on the ammeter it is necessary to have   4._____

     A. switch No. 2 open
     B. switch No. 4 closed
     C. switch No. 3 closed and switch No. 1 open
     D. switch No. 3 open and switch No. 1 closed

23

5. When current is flowing through the 10-ohm resistors, the voltmeter reading will be   5.___

    A.   100 volts   B.   60 volts   C.   40 volts   D.   24 volts

6. In this circuit the ammeter should have a scale range of at least zero to   6.___

    A.   1 ampere   B.   2 amperes   C.   3 amperes   D.   4 amperes

7. With the switches set for this circuit to take maximum current from the line, then the current through the fuse will be approximately   7.___

    A.   1 ampere   B.   2 amperes   C.   4 amperes   D.   10 amperes

8. The abbreviations I.D. and O.D. used in describing conduit directly refer to its   8.___

    A.   diameter   B.   length   C.   conductivity   D.   weight

9. To cut off a piece of #0000 insulated copper cable it is best to use   9.___

    A.   a hacksaw   B.   side-cutting pliers
    C.   an electrician's knife   D.   light nippers

10. Conduit is galvanized in order to   10.___

    A.   improve electrical conductivity   B.   protect it from corrosion
    C.   obtain a smooth surface   D.   insulate it

11. The best material for an electrical contact finger subjected to constant bending is   11.___

    A.   brass   B.   aluminum
    C.   tin   D.   phosphor bronze

12. One disadvantage of porcelain as an insulator is that it is   12.___

    A.   only good for low voltage
    B.   not satisfactory on a-c circuits
    C.   a brittle material
    D.   easily compressed

13. To vary the speed of a d-c motor-generator set, it would be necessary to   13.___

    A.   use a rheostat in the generator field
    B.   use a voltage regulator on the generator output
    C.   use a rheostat in the motor field
    D.   shift the brushes on the generator

14. The ordinary telephone transmitter contains granules of   14.___

    A.   sulphur   B.   carbon   C.   borax   D.   lucite

15. A stubby screwdriver is especially designed for turning screws   15.___

    A.   having a damaged screw slot
    B.   which are jammed tight
    C.   with stripped threads
    D.   inaccessible to a longer screwdriver

16. It is important to make certain a ladle does not contain water before using it to scoop up molten solder since the water may   16._____

    A. cause serious personal injury
    B. prevent the solder from sticking
    C. cool the solder
    D. dilute the solder

17. Steel helmets give workers the most protection from   17._____

    A. eye injuries
    C. fire
    B. falling objects
    D. electric shock

18. A slight coating of rust on small tools is best removed by   18._____

    A. applying a heavy coat of vaseline
    B. rubbing with kerosene and fine steel wool
    C. scraping with a sharp knife
    D. rubbing with a dry cloth

19. In the case of an auto-transformer, it is *INCORRECT* to say that   19._____

    A. the primary is insulated from the secondary
    B. a magnetic core is used
    C. a.c. is required
    D. it can be used for power purposes

20. The number 6-32 for a machine screw specifies the diameter and the   20._____

    A. length
    B. the number of threads per inch
    C. type of head
    D. hardness

21. It is undesirable to allow a soldering iron to overheat since this would cause   21._____

    A. softening of the copper tip
    B. hardening of the copper tip
    C. the soldering fumes to become poisonous
    D. damage to the tinned surface of the tip

22. To measure the small gap between relay contacts, it would be best to use a   22._____

    A. vernier caliper
    C. feeler gage
    B. depth gage
    D. micrometer

23. Acid is not a desirable flux to use in soldering small connections mainly because it   23._____

    A. is corrosive
    B. is expensive
    C. requires skill in handling
    D. requires a very hot iron

25

24. It is good practice to use standard electrician's pliers to 24.____

    A. tighten nuts
    B. remove insulation from a wire
    C. cut BX sheath
    D. shorten a wood screw

25. Three resistors having respective resistances of 12 ohms, 5 ohms, and 1 ohm are con- 25.____
nected in parallel. The combined resistance will be

    A. 18 ohms
    C. 4 ohms
    B. 6 ohms
    D. less than 1 ohm

26. The star drill is a multiple-pointed chisel used for drilling 26.____

    A. brass
    C. wood
    B. stone and concrete
    D. aluminum

27. A screwdriver in good condition should have a blade whose bottom edge is 27.____

    A. rounded
    C. chisel-shaped
    B. knife-sharp
    D. flat

28. From the standpoint of management, the most desirable characteristic in a newly 28.____
appointed helper would be

    A. the lack of outside personal interests
    B. the ability to keep to himself and away from the other employees
    C. the ability to satisfactorily perform his assigned duties
    D. eagerness to ask questions about all phases of the work

29. To provide transit employees with quick assistance in the case of minor injuries it would 29.____
be most logical to

    A. instruct the employees in first-aid techniques
    B. provide each employee with a first-aid kit
    C. have one centrally located medical office for the transit system
    D. equip all employees with walkie-talkie devices

30. One result of corrosion of an electrical connection is that 30.____

    A. its resistance increases
    B. its resistance decreases
    C. its temperature drops
    D. the current in the circuit increases

31. Subway cars are equipped with storage batteries. These batteries are *LEAST* likely to be 31.___
used to supply power to the car

    A. traction motors
    B. emergency lights
    C. public address system
    D. motorman-conductor communication system

32. The size of a screwdriver is defined by the   32._____

    A. length of the handle   B. thickness of the blade
    C. length of the blade   D. diameter of the handle

33. A newly appointed helper would be expected to do his work in the manner prescribed by   33._____
his foreman because

    A. it insures discipline
    B. good results are more certain with less supervision
    C. no other method would work
    D. it permits speed-up

34. When a soldered splice is covered with both rubber and friction tape, the main function of   34._____
the friction tape is to

    A. provide extra electrical insulation
    B. protect the rubber tape
    C. make the splice water-tight
    D. increase the mechanical strength of the splice

35. Powdered graphite is a good   35._____

    A. lubricant   B. abrasive   C. adhesive   D. insulator

36. A zero adjusting screw will be found on most   36._____

    A. overload relays   B. lightning arrestors
    C. voltmeters   D. switches

37. Lock nuts are frequently used in making electrical connections on terminal boards. The   37._____
purpose of the lock-nuts is to

    A. keep the connections from loosening through vibration
    B. prevent unauthorized personnel from tampering with the connections
    C. eliminate the use of flat washers
    D. increase the contact area at the connection point

38. The abbreviation D.P.D.T. used in electrical work describes a type of   38._____

    A. switch   B. motor   C. fuse   D. generator

39. A wire has a resistance of 2 ohms per 1000 feet. A piece of this wire 1500 feet long will   39._____
have a resistance of

    A. 1 ohm   B. 1.5 ohms   C. 2.5 ohms   D. 3 ohms

40. The dielectric strength of the oil used in an oil filled transformer is a direct measure of the   40._____
oil's

    A. viscosity   B. weight
    C. breakdown voltage   D. current carrying capacity

41. The power fed to a mercury arc rectifier would probably come from   41.___

    A. a rotary converter   B. a d.c.generator
    C. an a.c.source   D. a battery

42. The ordinary plug fuse has   42.___

    A. knife blade contacts   B. screw base contacts
    C. ferrule contacts   D. jack contacts

43. When using a hacksaw, it is good practice to   43.___

    A. tighten the blade in the frame by using pliers on the wing nut
    B. use heavy pressure on both the forward and return strokes
    C. slow the speed of cutting when the piece is almost cut through
    D. use very short, very rapid strokes

44. A new helper is told by an experienced helper that he is not doing a particular job prop-   44.___
erly. The best reason for the new helper to give this advice due consideration is that the
other helper

    A. has the authority to enforce his advice
    B. has more experience on the job
    C. will be resentful if his advice is not taken
    D. will not help the new man again if his advice is not taken

45. The main purpose of the oil in an oil circuit breaker is to   45.___

    A. quench the arc   B. lubricate the moving parts
    C. prevent corrosion   D. absorb moisture

46. A piece of electrical equipment which does NOT require a magnetic field for its operation   46.___
is

    A. a motor   B. a generator
    C. a transformer   D. an electrostatic voltmeter

47. The rating term "20-watts, 500-ohm" would generally be applied to a   47.___

    A. resistor   B. condenser
    C. switch   D. circuit breaker

48. The core of an electro-magnet is usually made of   48.___

    A. lead   B. iron   C. brass   D. bakelite

49. The A.W.G. size is used in specifying   49.___

    A. wires   B. condensers   C. switches   D. fuses

50. The metal which is preferred for use in relay contacts is   50.___

    A. brass   B. tin   C. silver   D. aluminum

KEY (CORRECT ANSWERS)

1.	A	11.	D	21.	D	31.	A	41.	C
2.	D	12.	C	22.	C	32.	C	42.	B
3.	D	13.	C	23.	A	33.	B	43.	C
4.	B	14.	B	24.	B	34.	B	44.	B
5.	D	15.	D	25.	D	35.	A	45.	A
6.	D	16.	A	26.	B	36.	C	46.	D
7.	D	17.	B	27.	D	37.	A	47.	A
8.	A	18.	B	28.	C	38.	A	48.	B
9.	A	19.	A	29.	A	39.	D	49.	A
10.	B	20.	B	30.	A	40.	C	50.	C

29

EXAMINATION SECTION
TEST 1

DIRECTIONS: Each question or incomplete statement Is followed by several suggested answers or completions. Select the one that *BEST* answers the question or completes the statement. *PRINT THE LETTER OF THE CORRECT ANSWER IN THE SPACE AT THE RIGHT.*

1. A good magnetic material is

   A. aluminum   B. iron   C. brass   D. carbon

1.____

2. A thermo-couple is a device for

   A. changing frequency
   B. changing d.c. to a.c.
   C. measuring temperature
   D. heat insulation

2.____

3. It is desired to operate a 6-volt lamp from a 120-volt a.c. source. This can be done with the least waste power by using a

   A. series resistor   B. rectifier
   C. step-down transformer   D. rheostat

3.____

4. Rosin is a material generally used

   A. in batteries
   B. as a dielectric
   C. as a soldering flux
   D. for high voltage insulation

4.____

5. A milliampere is

   A. 1000 amperes   B. 100 amperes
   C. .01 ampere   D. .001 ampere

5.____

6. A compound motor usually has

   A. only a shunt field
   B. only a series field
   C. no brushes
   D. both a shunt and a series field

6.____

7. To connect a d.c. voltmeter to measure a voltage higher than the scale maximum, use a

   A. series resistance   B. shunt
   C. current transformer   D. voltage transformer

7.____

8. The voltage applied to the terminals of a storage battery to charge it *CANNOT* be

   A. rectified a.c.   B. straight d.c.
   C. pulsating d.c.   D. ordinary a.c.

8.____

9. When two unequal condensers are connected in parallel, the

9.____

A. total capacity is decreased
B. total capacity is increased
C. result will be a short-circuit
D. smaller one will break down

10. A megohm is   10.____

    A. 10 ohms   B. 100 ohms
    C. 1000 ohms   D. 1,000,000 ohms

11. Of the following, the *POOREST* conductor of electricity is   11.____

    A. brass   B. lead
    C. an acid solution   D. slate

12. A flashlight battery, a condenser and a flashlight bulb are connected in series with each   12.____
other. If the bulb burns brightly and steadily, then the condenser is

    A. open-circuited   B. short-circuited
    C. good   D. fully charged

13. A kilowatt of power will be taken from a 500-volt d.c. supply by a load of   13.____

    A. 200 amperes   B. 20 amperes
    C. 2 amperes   D. 0.2 ampere

14. A commutator is used on a shunt generator in order to   14.____

    A. step-up voltage   B. step-up current
    C. change a.c. to d.c.   D. control generator speed

15. The number of cells connected in series in a 6-volt storage battery of the lead-acid type   15.____
is

    A. 2   B. 3   C. 4   D. 5

16. A 15-ampere circuit breaker as compared to a 15-ampere plug fuse   16.____

    A. can be re-closed   B. is cheaper
    C. is safer   D. is smaller

17. Lengths of rigid conduit are connected together to make up a long run by means of   17.____

    A. couplings   B. bushings
    C. hickeys   D. lock nuts

18. BX is commonly used to indicate   18.____

    A. rigid conduit without wires
    B. flexible conduit without wires
    C. insulated wires covered with flexible steel armor
    D. insulated wires covered with a non-metallic covering

19. Good practice is to cut BX with a   19.____

    A. hacksaw   B. 3-wheel pipe cutter
    C. bolt cutter   D. heavy pliers

20. Silver is used for relay contacts in order to   20.____

A. improve conductivity
B. avoid burning
C. reduce costs
D. avoid arcing

21. Rigid conduit is fastened on the inside of the junction box by means of   21.____

    A. a bushing
    B. a locknut
    C. a coupling
    D. set-screw clamps

22. Of the following, the material which can best withstand high temperatures is   22.____

    A. plastic   B. enamel   C. fiber   D. mica

23. A lead-acid type of storage battery exposed to freezing weather is most likely to freeze   23.____
    when

    A. the battery is fully charged
    B. the battery is completely discharged
    C. the water level is low
    D. the cap vent holes are plugged

24. An important reason making it poor practice to put telephone wires in the same conduit   24.____
    with a.c. power lines is that

    A. power will be lost from the a.c. line
    B. the conduit will overheat
    C. the wires may be confused
    D. the telephone circuits will be noisy

25. In a loaded power circuit, it is most dangerous to   25.____

    A. close the circuit with a circuit breaker
    B. close the circuit with a knife switch
    C. open the circuit with a knife switch
    D. open the circuit with a circuit breaker

26. When fastening electrical equipment to a hollow tile wall it is good practice to use   26.____

    A. toggle bolts
    B. wood screws
    C. nails
    D. ordinary bolts and nuts

27. Of the following, the most important reason for keeping the oil in a transformer tank mois-   27.____
    ture-free is to prevent

    A. rusting
    B. voltage breakdown
    C. freezing of the oil
    D. overheating

28. A voltmeter is generally connected to a high potential a.c. bus through   28.____

    A. an auto-transformer
    B. a potential transformer
    C. a resistor
    D. a relay

29. The highest total voltage which can be measured by using two identical 0-300 volt range   29.____
    meters connected in series would be

    A. 150 volts
    B. 300 volts
    C. 450 volts
    D. 600 volts

30. Transistors are mainly employed in electrical circuits to take the place of   30.____

33

A.   resistors
C.   inductances

B.   condensers
D.   vacuum tubes

31.   The minimum number of 10-ohm, 1-ampere resistors which would be required to give an   31.___
equivalent resistance of 10 ohms capable of carrying a 2-ampere load is

A.   2   B.   3   C.   4   D.   5

32.   To increase the current measuring range of an ammeter, the equipment commonly   32.___
employed is a

A.   series resistor
B.   shunt
C.   short-circuiting switch
D.   choke

33.   If a 10-watt lamp and a 100-watt lamp, each rated at 120 volts, are connected in series to   33.___
a 240-volt source, then the voltage across the 10-watt lamp will be

A.   zero
B.   about 24 volts
C.   exactly 120 volts
D.   much more than 120 volts

34.   If the load on the secondary of a small 10 to 1 step-up transformer is 100 watts, then the   34.___
power being taken by the primary from the power line

A.   is less than 100 watts
B.   is exactly 100 watts
C.   is more than 100 watts
D.   may be more or less than 100 watts depending on the nature of the load

35.   A 1/2-ohm, a 2-ohm, a 5-ohm and a 25-ohm resistor are connected in series to a power   35.___
source. The resistor which will consume the most power is the

A.   1/2-ohm   B.   2-ohm   C.   5-ohm   D.   25-ohm

36.   With respect to 60-cycle current, it is correct to say that one cycle takes   36.___

A.   1/60th of a second
C.   1/60th of a minute

B.   1/30th of a second
D.   1/30th of a minute

37.   A rheostat is used in the field circuit of a shunt generator to control the   37.___

A.   generator speed
C.   generator voltage

B.   load
D.   power factor

Questions 38-45.
Questions 38 through 45 are based on the Subway Power Supply Information given below.
Read this information carefully before answering these questions.

SUBWAY POWER SUPPLY INFORMATION

The subway train signal system derives its power from a 3-phase, 4-wire, 60-cycle a.c. source which has a phase to phase voltage of 208 volts and a voltage of 120 volts between each phase wire and the grounded neutral. The signal system power is taken from one phase wire and the grounded neutral and applied to the primary of a 1 to 1 transformer. The secondary of this transformer powers the signal main. Train propulsion power is 600 volts supplied from mercury arc rectifiers and fed to the 3rd rail, from which it is picked up by car contact shoes, taken through the car motors as required and returned through the car wheels and then through one of the running rails back to the power source. This rail, known as the negative propulsion current rail, has heavy bonds around each rail joint. The other running rail, known as the signal rail, has insulated rail joints at various intervals to separate one track signal circuit from another and the rail joints between insulated joints are bonded with relatively light bonds.

38. The voltage on the signal main is most nearly   38._____

     A. 600 volts d.c.   B. 208 volts a.c.
     C. 120 volts a.c.   D. 120 volts d.c.

39. The voltage on the contact shoes of the car is   39._____

     A. 600 volts d.c.   B. 600 volts a.c.
     C. 208 volts a.c.   D. 120 volts d.c.

40. It is apparent that the number of conductors in a signal main is   40._____

     A. one   B. two   C. three   D. four

41. Since the 1 to 1 transformer does not change the voltage, its purpose is to insulate   41._____

     A. the signal main from the 600-volt supply
     B. the signal main from the 3-phase source
     C. adjacent track circuits
     D. the 3rd rail from the running rail

42. Light bonds are provided on the rail joints of   42._____

     A. the 3rd rail
     B. both running rails
     C. one running rail
     D. the negative propulsion current rail

43. Track signal circuits are separated from other by   43._____

     A. rail bonds   B. ordinary rail joints
     C. a grounded neutral   D. insulated rail joints

44. The negative return for the car motors is through   44._____

     A. the 3rd rail   B. the signal rail
     C. both running rails   D. one running rail

45. If one insulated rail joint becomes short-circuited, then the number of track signal circuits   45._____
    affected will be

     A. one   B. two   C. three   D. four

46. If a condenser has a safe working voltage of 250 volts d.c., then it would be most likely to break down if used across

    A. a 250-volt, 60-cycle a.c. line
    B. a 250-volt d.c. line
    C. a 240-volt battery
    D. a 120-volt, 25-cycle a.c. line

46.___

47. Transformer cores are generally made up of thin steel laminations. The main purpose of this is to

    A. reduce the transformer losses
    B. reduce the initial cost of the transformer
    C. increase the weight of the transformer
    D. prevent voltage breakdown in the transformer

47.___

48. The main reason for using copper tips in soldering irons is because copper

    A. is a good heat conductor
    B. is a good electrical conductor
    C. has a low melting point
    D. is very soft

48.___

49. Five identical electric fans, each rated at 120 volts d.c. are connected in series with each other on a 600-volt circuit. If one fan develops an open circuit then

    A. the remaining fans will run, but at slow speed
    B. the remaining fans will run, but at above normal speed
    C. only one fan will run
    D. none of the fans will run

49.___

50. The pressure of a carbon brush on a commutator is measured with a

    A. spring balance   B. feeler gage
    C. taper gage   D. wire gage

50.___

KEY (CORRECT ANSWERS)

1. B	11. D	21. A	31. C	41. B
2. C	12. B	22. D	32. B	42. C
3. C	13. C	23. B	33. D	43. D
4. C	14. C	24. D	34. C	44. D
5. D	15. B	25. C	35. D	45. B
6. D	16. A	26. A	36. A	46. A
7. A	17. A	27. B	37. C	47. A
8. D	18. C	28. B	38. C	48. A
9. B	19. A	29. D	39. A	49. D
10. D	20. A	30. D	40. B	50. A

TEST 2

DIRECTIONS: Each question or incomplete statement is followed by several suggested answers or completions. Select the one that BEST answers the question or completes the statement. *PRINT THE LETTER OF THE CORRECT ANSWER IN THE SPACE AT THE RIGHT.*

1. A non-inductive carbon resistor consumes 50 watts when connected across a 120-volt d.c. source. If it is connected across a 120-volt a.c. source, the power consumed by the resistor will be nearest to

    A. 30 watts   B. 40 watts   C. 50 watts   D. 60 watts

1.____

2. Of the following, the combination of lamps which will draw the most current from a standard 120-volt branch circuit is one with

    A. three 150-watt lamps   B. one 300-watt lamp
    C. four 100-watt lamps   D. six 50-watt lamps

2.____

3. A condenser is sometimes connected across contact points which make and break a d.c. circuit in order to reduce arcing of the points. The condenser produces this effect because it

    A. discharges when the contacts open
    B. charges when the contacts open
    C. charges while the contacts are closed
    D. discharges when the contacts are closed

3.____

4. One of the difficulties experienced with d.c. motors is "high mica." To correct this trouble, good practice is to

    A. use very soft commutator bars
    B. use very soft brushes
    C. undercut the mica
    D. use very narrow commutator bars

4.____

5. A 120-volt a.c. generator has a full load rating of 12 kva. This means that full load current for this machine is

    A. 10 amperes   B. 100 amperes
    C. 1000 amperes   D. 10,000 amperes

5.____

6. A power-factor meter would be used in

    A. a battery circuit
    B. a d.c. generator circuit
    C. an a.c. generator circuit
    D. a d.c. motor circuit

6.____

7. Measurements of the air-gap clearance between the pole pieces and the armature of a motor are useful in determining wear of the

    A. commutator   B. brushes
    C. bearings   D. pole pieces

7.____

8. Transit workers are cautioned not to leave tools on scaffolding. The most important reason for this rule is to

    A. prevent theft of the tools
    B. prevent mix-ups in the worker's tools
    C. prevent damage to tools
    D. avoid a safety hazard

8.___

9. Transit workers are advised to report injuries caused by nails, no matter how slight. The most important reason for this rule is that this type of injury

    A. is caused by violating safety rules
    B. can only be caused by carelessness
    C. generally causes dangerous bleeding
    D. may result in a serious infection

9.___

10. In connection with the use of a wire snale, it is *NOT* necessary to

    A. tape it when coiled
    B. avoid kinking
    C. grease it
    D. avoid contact with live circuits

10.___

11. The material discharged by a carbon dioxide fire extinguisher should not be handled because it

    A. can cause a frost-bite
    B. is a poisonous liquid
    C. is highly volatile
    D. is valuable for re-use

11.___

12. Aluminum is often used for transmission lines instead of copper because it

    A. is stronger
    B. is lighter
    C. has higher conductivity
    D. is non-corrosive

12.___

13. The colored lenses on the subway signals located along the trackway are replaced as quickly as possible if they are broken. The most important reason for doing this is probably to prevent

    A. misunderstanding of the signal by a motorman
    B. injuries from broken glass
    C. the signal lamp from burning out too quickly
    D. dirt from getting on the signal lamp

13.___

14. An important precaution in connection with electric welding is to

    A. avoid shock
    B. prevent overloading the machine
    C. protect the face and eyes
    D. wear loose clothes

14.___

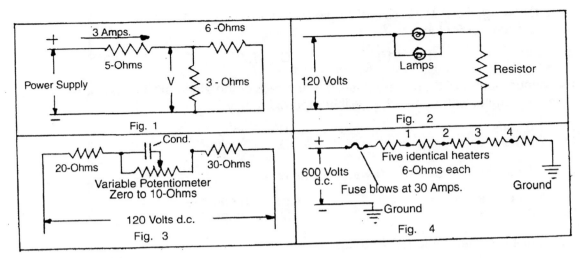

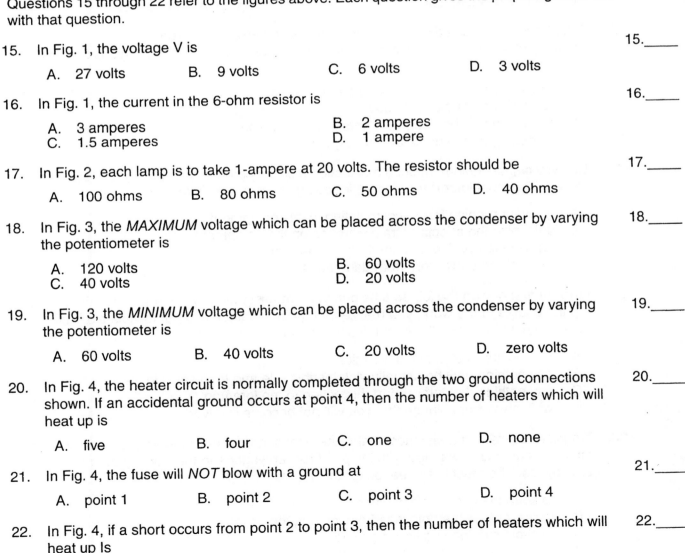

Questions 15 - 22 .
Questions 15 through 22 refer to the figures above. Each question gives the proper figure to use with that question.

15. In Fig. 1, the voltage V is

    A.   27 volts   B.   9 volts   C.   6 volts   D.   3 volts

15.____

16. In Fig. 1, the current in the 6-ohm resistor is

    A.   3 amperes   B.   2 amperes
    C.   1.5 amperes   D.   1 ampere

16.____

17. In Fig. 2, each lamp is to take 1-ampere at 20 volts. The resistor should be

    A.   100 ohms   B.   80 ohms   C.   50 ohms   D.   40 ohms

17.____

18. In Fig. 3, the *MAXIMUM* voltage which can be placed across the condenser by varying the potentiometer is

    A.   120 volts   B.   60 volts
    C.   40 volts   D.   20 volts

18.____

19. In Fig. 3, the *MINIMUM* voltage which can be placed across the condenser by varying the potentiometer is

    A.   60 volts   B.   40 volts   C.   20 volts   D.   zero volts

19.____

20. In Fig. 4, the heater circuit is normally completed through the two ground connections shown. If an accidental ground occurs at point 4, then the number of heaters which will heat up is

    A.   five   B.   four   C.   one   D.   none

20.____

21. In Fig. 4, the fuse will *NOT* blow with a ground at

    A.   point 1   B.   point 2   C.   point 3   D.   point 4

21.____

22. In Fig. 4, if a short occurs from point 2 to point 3, then the number of heaters which will heat up Is

    A.   five   B.   four   C.   two   D.   none

22.____

23. Of the following, the A.W.G. size of single conductor bare copper wire which has the low-   23.___
    est resistance per foot is

    A. #40   B. #10   C. #00   D. #0

24. The voltage output of 6 ordinary flashlight dry cells of the zinc-carbon type, when con-   24.___
    nected in parallel with each other, will be approximately

    A. 1.5 volts   B. 3 volts
    C. 9 volts   D. 12 volts

25. Full load current for a 5-ohm, 20-watt resistor is   25.___

    A. 4 amperes   B. 3 amperes
    C. 2 amperes   D. 1 ampere

26. An auto-transformer could *NOT* be used to   26.___

    A. step-up voltage   B. step-down voltage
    C. act as a choke coil   D. change a.c. frequency

27. Telephones are located alongside of the subway tracks for emergency use. The locations   27.___
    of these telephones are indicated by blue lights. The reason for selecting this color rather
    than green is that

    A. a blue light can be seen for greater distances
    B. blue lights are easier to buy
    C. green cannot be seen by a person who is colorblind
    D. green lights are used for train signals

28. Subway signal equipment such as junction boxes located in the subway are kept pad-   28.___
    locked. The most important reason, for doing this is probably to

    A. prevent rubbish from accumulating in this equipment
    B. minimize the effects of train vibration on the equipment
    C. prevent tampering by unauthorized personnel
    D. protect the equipment from dampness

29. On your first day on the job as a helper, you are assigned to work with a maintainer. Dur- 29.___
    ing the course of the work, you realize that the maintainer is about to violate a basic
    safety rule. In this case the best thing for you to do is to

    A. immediately call it to his attention
    B. say nothing until he actually violates this rule and then call it to his attention
    C. say nothing, but later report this action to the foreman
    D. walk away from him so that you will not become involved

30. Transit rules state that electrical maintainers must not permit other employees to replace 30.___
    lamps of authorized wattage with lamps of higher wattage in the working areas of such
    employees. The most likely reason for this rule is

    A. to keep the cost of electricity down
    B. to prevent such employees from injuring their eyes
    C. to avoid overloading lighting circuits
    D. that higher wattage lamps cost more

31. If you find that the fuse clip on one side of a fuse is much hotter than the fuse clip on the other side of this fuse, it would indicate   31._____

    A. that the fuse is rated too low
    B. that the fuse is rated too high
    C. that the load current is too high
    D. poor contact at the hot fuse clip

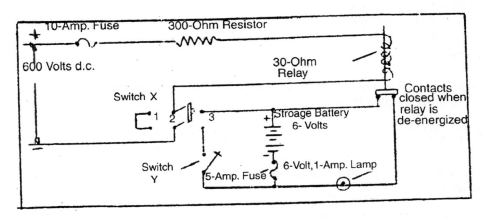

Questions 32 - 39.
Questions 32 through 39 are based on the above wiring diagram. Refer to this diagram when answering these questions.

32. Throwing switch X to Position No. 1 will   32._____

    A. charge the battery   B. energize the lamp
    C. energize the relay   D. blow the 5-ampere fuse

33. With switch X in Position No. 1, the 10-ampere fuse will blow if a dead short occurs across the   33._____

    A. 300-ohm resistor   B. relay coil
    C. battery   D. lamp

34. With switch X in Position No. 2, the current through the 300-ohm resistor will be   34._____

    A. zero   B. 2 amperes
    C. 2.2 amperes   D. 10 amperes

35. With switch X in Position No. 3, and switch Y open, the current taken from the battery will be   35._____

    A. zero   B. 1 ampere
    C. 5 amperes   D. 10 amperes

36. With switch Y in the open position and the relay contacts open,   36._____

    A. the lamp will be lit
    B. the lamp will be dark
    C. the battery will be discharging
    D. the 5-ampere fuse will be overloaded

37. The battery will charge with   37._____

A. switch X in Position No. 3 and switch Y closed
B. switch X in Position No. 3 and switch Y open
C. switch X in Position No. 1 and switch Y closed
D. switch X in Position No. 1 and switch Y open

38. With the relay contacts closed, a dead short across the lamp will   38.___

    A. blow the 10-ampere fuse
    B. blow the 5-ampere fuse
    C. not blow any fuses
    D. cause the battery to charge

39. When the switches are set to the positions which will charge the battery, the charging   39.___
current will be approximately

    A. 1/2 ampere   B. 2 amperes
    C. 5 amperes   D. 10 amperes

40. The most important reason for *NOT* having a power line splice in a conduit run between   40.___
boxes is that

    A. it will be impossible to pull the wires through
    B. this would be an unsafe practice
    C. the splice will heat up
    D. the splice would be hard to repair

41. Goggles would be *LEAST* necessary when   41.___

    A. recharging soda-acid fire extinguishers
    B. clipping stones
    C. putting electrolyte into an Edison battery
    D. scraping rubber insulation from a wire

42. A commutator and brushes will be found on   42.___

    A. an alternator
    B. a rotary converter
    C. a squirrel-cage induction motor
    D. a wound-rotor induction motor

43. In a house bell circuit, the push button for ringing the bell is generally connected in the   43.___
secondary of the transformer feeding the bell. One reason for doing this is to

    A. save power
    B. keep line voltage out of the push button circuit
    C. prevent the bell from burning out
    D. prevent arcing of the vibrator contact points in the bell

44. If a 120-volt transformer is connected to a 120-volt d.c. source, then the   44.___

    A. secondary voltage will cause the transformer to break down
    B. secondary current will be excessive
    C. primary current will cause the transformer to overheat
    D. primary voltage will be too low for the transformer to operate properly

45. The Wheatstone Bridge which is used for measuring resistances has   45.____

    A. a galvanometer   B. a wattmeter
    C. a foot-candle meter   D. a frequency meter

46. A wire has a resistance of 1 ohm per 1000 feet. A piece of this wire 200 feet long will   46.____
have a resistance of

    A. .002 ohm   B. .02 ohm   C. .2 ohm   D. .5 ohm

47. The lead sheath of a cable is for the purpose of protecting the cable from   47.____

    A. water damage   B. temperature changes
    C. eddy currents   D. kinking

48. There are only a few emergency lights provided for subway car illumination, when the   48.____
main lights go out because of loss of 3rd rail power. The best reason for providing only a
few emergency lights is that these lamps

    A. are fed from a battery supply
    B. burn for longer periods than the main lights
    C. are more difficult to replace than the main lights
    D. provide as much light as the main lights

49. Before conducting an insulation resistance test on large machines with a megger, it is   49.____
considered good practice to ground the windings for about 15 minutes immediately prior
to the test. The most likely reason for this is to

    A. allow the machine to cool down
    B. remove static electricity which may have accumulated during the running of the
        machine
    C. reduce hazard from lightning
    D. permit moisture to evaporate from the windings

50. Sediment in the cells of a storage battery will most likely tend to   50.____

    A. increase the voltage output
    B. increase the current output
    C. short the cells
    D. cause the battery to leak

KEY (CORRECT ANSWERS)

1.	C	11.	A	21.	D	31.	D	41.	D
2.	A	12.	B	22.	B	32.	C	42.	B
3.	B	13.	A	23.	C	33.	A	43.	B
4.	C	14.	C	24.	A	34.	A	44.	C
5.	B	15.	C	25.	C	35.	B	45.	A
6.	C	16.	D	26.	D	36.	B	46.	C
7.	C	17.	C	27.	D	37.	A	47.	A
8.	D	18.	D	28.	C	38.	B	48.	A
9.	D	19.	D	29.	A	39.	B	49.	B
10.	C	20.	B	30.	C	40.	B	50.	C

———

EXAMINATION SECTION
TEST 1

DIRECTIONS: Each question or incomplete statement is followed by several suggested answers or completions. Select the one that *BEST* answers the question or completes the statement. *PRINT THE LETTER OF THE CORRECT ANSWER IN THE SPACE AT THE RIGHT.*

1. A circular mil is a measure of

    A. area   B. length   C. volume   D. weight

1._____

2. In electrical tests, a megger is calibrated to read

    A. amperes   B. ohms   C. volts   D. watts

2._____

3. Metal cabinets for lighting circuits are grounded in order to

    A. save insulating material
    B. provide a return for the neutral current
    C. eliminate short circuits
    D. minimize the possibility of shock

3._____

4. In an a.c. circuit containing only resistance, the power factor will be

    A. zero   B. 50% lagging
    C. 50% leading   D. 100%

4._____

5. The size of fuse for a two-wire lighting circuit using No. 14 wire should not exceed

    A. 15 amperes   B. 20 amperes
    C. 25 amperes   D. 30 amperes

5._____

6. When working near acid storage batteries, extreme care should be taken to guard against sparks mainly because a spark may

    A. cause an explosion
    B. set fire to the electrolyte
    C. short circuit a cell
    D. ignite the battery case

6._____

7. If a blown fuse in an existing lighting circuit is replaced by another of the same rating which also blows, the proper maintenance procedure is to

    A. use a higher rating fuse
    B. cut out some of the outlets in the circuit
    C. check the circuit for grounds or shorts
    D. install a renewable fuse

7._____

8. The number of fuses required in a three-phase four-wire branch circuit with grounded neutral is

    A. one   B. two   C. three   D. four

8._____

9. The electrodes of the common dry cell are carbon and

    A. zinc   B. lead   C. steel   D. tin

9._____

10. An electrician's hickey is used to   10.____

    A. strip insulation off wire
    B. pull cable through conduits
    C. thread metallic conduit
    D. bend metallic conduit

11. A group of wire sizes that is correctly arranged in order of *INCREASING* current-carrying   11.____
capacity is

    A. 6; 12; 3/0   B. 12; 6; 3/0
    C. 3/0; 12; 6   D. 3/0; 6; 12

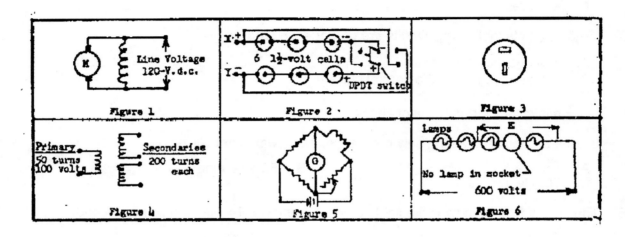

Questions 12 - 19.
Questions 12 through 19 refer to the figures above. Each question gives the proper figure
to use with that question.

12. Figure 1 shows the standard diagram for   12.____

    A. a synchronous motor   B. a shunt motor
    C. a series motor   D. an induction motor

13. In Figure 1, if the line current is 5 amperes, the energy consumed by the motor if in con-   13.____
tinuous operation for 3 hours is

    A. 200 watthours   B. 600 watthours
    C. 1800 watthours   D. 9000 watthours

14. In Figure 2, with the DPDT switch closed to the right, the voltage between X and Y is   14.____

    A. 0   B. 1 1/2   C. 4 1/2   D. 9

15. In Figure 2, with the DPDT closed to the left, the voltage between X and Y is   15.____

    A. 9   B. 4 1/2   C. 1 1/2   D. 0

16. The convenience outlet shown in Figure 3 is used particularly for a device which   16.____

    A. is polarized   B. is often disconnected
    C. takes a heavy current   D. vibrates

17. In Figure 4, the *MAXIMUM* secondary voltage possible by interconnecting the secondaries is   17.____

    A. 50 volts   B. 200 volts
    C. 400 volts   D. 800 volts

18. Figure 5 shows a Wheatstone bridge which is used to measure   18.____

    A. voltage   B. resistance
    C. current   D. power

19. In Figure 6, with one of the five good lamps removed from its socket as indicated, the voltage is nearest to   19.____

    A. 240   B. 0   C. 600   D. 360

20. The metal which is the best conductor of electricity is   20.____

    A. silver   B. copper
    C. aluminum   D. nickel

21. If the two supply wires to a d.c. series motor are reversed, the motor will   21.____

    A. run in the opposite direction
    B. not run
    C. run in the same direction
    D. become a generator

22. Before doing work on a motor, to prevent accidental starting you should   22.____

    A. short circuit the motor leads
    B. remove the fuses
    C. block the rotor
    D. ground the frame

23. The material commonly used for brushes on d.c. motors is   23.____

    A. copper   B. carbon
    C. brass   D. aluminum

24. The conductors of a two-wire No. 12 armored cable used in an ordinary lighting circuit are   24.____

    A. stranded and rubber insulated
    B. solid and rubber insulated
    C. stranded and cotton insulated
    D. solid and cotton insulated

25. The rating, 125 V.-10A., 250 V.-5A., commonly applies to a   25.____

    A. snap switch   B. lamp
    C. conductor   D. fuse

26. Commutators are found on   26.____

    A. alternators   B. d.c. motors
    C. transformers   D. circuit breakers

27. A proper use for an electrician's knife is to   27.____

    A. cut wires
    B. pry out a small cartridge fuse
    C. mark the placd where a conduit is to be cut
    D. skin wires

28. A d.c. device taking one milliampere at one kilovolt takes a total power of   28.____

    A. one milliwatt   B. one watt
    C. one kilowatt   D. one megawatt

29. In connection with electrical work, it is good practice to   29.____

    A. scrape the silvery coating from a wire before soldering
    B. nick a wire in several places before bending it around a terminal
    C. assume that a circuit is alive
    D. open a switch to check the load

30. Mica is commonly used as an insulation   30.____

    A. for cartridge fuse cases
    B. between commutator bars
    C. between lead acid battery plates
    D. between transformer steel laminations

31. The function of a step-down transformer is to decrease the   31.____

    A. voltage   B. current
    C. power   D. frequency

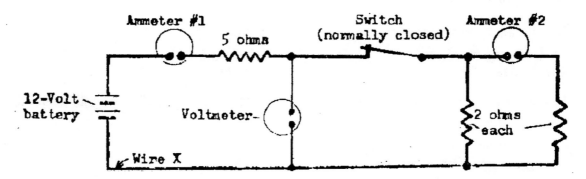

Questions 32-39.
Questions 32 through 39 refer to the circuit above. Neglect the effects of the various meters on the circuit.

32. The three resistors connected as shown have an equivalent resistance of   32.____

    A. 9 ohms   B. 7 ohms   C. 6 ohms   D. 4 ohms

33. When ammeter #1 indicates 2 amperes, ammeter #2 will indicate   33.____

    A. 1 ampere   B. 2 amperes
    C. 3 amperes   D. 4 amperes

34. If the two wires to ammeter #1 are reversed the

    A.   ammeter needle will move backwards
    B.   ammeter needle will indicate zero
    C.   ammeter will burn out
    D.   current in the rest of the circuit will be reversed

34.____

35. With the switch either open or closed, the current in wire X is

    A.   greater than in ammeter #1
    B.   less than in ammeter #1
    C.   the same as in ammeter #2
    D.   the same as in ammeter #1

35.____

36. When ammeter #1 indicates 2 amperes, the power consumed by the 5-ohm resistor is

    A.   2.5 watts   B.   10 watts
    C.   20 watts   D.   50 watts

36.____

37. The highest voltage measured anywhere in the circuit is across the

    A.   5-ohm resistor   B.   No. 1 ammeter
    C.   battery   D.   closed switch

37.____

38. If the normally-closed switch is opened, the meter that would still show an appreciable reading is

    A.   the voltmeter   B.   ammeter #1
    C.   ammeter #2   D.   none

38.____

39. The device in the circuit which undoubtedly has the highest resistance is the

    A.   battery   B.   5-ohm resistor
    C.   No. 1 ammeter   D.   voltmeter

39.____

40. A conduit run is most often terminated in

    A.   a coupling   B.   an elbow
    C.   a bushing   D.   an outlet box

40.____

41. In long conduit runs, pull boxes are sometimes installed at intermediate points to

    A.   avoid using couplings
    B.   support the conduit
    C.   make use of short lengths of conduit
    D.   facilitate pulling wire

41.____

42. A rheostat would *LEAST* likely be used in connection with the operation of

    A.   transformers   B.   motors
    C.   generators   D.   battery charging M.G. sets

42.____

43. The fiber bushing inserted at the end of a piece of flexible metallic conduit prevents

    A.   moisture from entering the cable
    B.   the rough edges from cutting the insulation
    C.   the wires from touching each other
    D.   the wires from slipping back into the armor

43.____

44. Portable lamp cord is most likely to have   44.____

    A. paper insulation   B. solid wire
    C. armored wire   D. stranded wire

45. Thermal relays are used in motor circuits to protect against   45.____

    A. reverse current   B. overspeed
    C. overvoltage   D. overload

46. It is good practice to connect the ground wire for a building electrical system to a   46.____

    A. vent pipe   B. steam pipe
    C. cold water pipe   D. gas pipe

47. A good magnetic material is   47.____

    A. brass   B. copper   C. silver   D. iron

48. The most practical way to determine in the field the approximate length of insulated wire   48.____
in a large coil is to

    A. unreel the wire and measure it with a 6-foot rule
    B. find another coil with the length marked on it and compare
    C. count the turns and multiply by the average circumference
    D. weigh the coil and compare it with a 1000-ft. coil

49. When the connections for a d.c. voltmeter are moved from one test point to another, the   49.____
needle moves backwards. This means that the

    A. second test point is a.c.
    B. meter is defective
    C. meter is magnetized
    D. meter leads are reversed

50. A good insulating material that can be machined readily to a required shape is   50.____

    A. mica   B. porcelain
    C. bakelite   D. varnished cambric

KEY (CORRECT ANSWERS)

1.	A	11.	B	21.	C	31.	A	41.	D
2.	B	12.	B	22.	B	32.	C	42.	A
3.	D	13.	C	23.	B	33.	A	43.	B
4.	D	14.	C	24.	B	34.	A	44.	D
5.	A	15.	A	25.	A	35.	D	45.	D
6.	A	16.	A	26.	B	36.	C	46.	C
7.	C	17.	D	27.	D	37.	C	47.	D
8.	C	18.	B	28.	B	38.	A	48.	C
9.	A	19.	C	29.	C	39.	D	49.	D
10.	D	20.	A	30.	B	40.	D	50.	C

TEST 2

DIRECTIONS: Each question or incomplete statement is followed by several suggested answers or completions. Select the one that *BEST* answers the question or completes the statement. *PRINT THE LETTER OF THE CORRECT ANSWER IN THE SPACE AT THE RIGHT.*

1. In most cases, the logical and proper source from which you should first seek explanation of one of the transit rules you do not understand would be the   1._____

    A.   Transit Authority
    B.   head of your department
    C.   maintainer with whom you are assigned to work
    D.   helper who has an assignment similar to your own

2. Employees of the transit system whose work requires them to enter upon the tracks in the subway are cautioned not to wear loose fitting clothing. The *MOST* important reason for this caution is that loose fitting clothing may   2._____

    A.   interfere when men are using heavy tools
    B.   catch on some projection of a passing train
    C.   tear more easily than snug fitting clothing
    D.   give insufficient protection against subway dust

3. Your work will probably be *MOST* appreciated by your superior if you show that   3._____

    A.   you like your work by asking all the questions you can about it
    B.   you're on the job by keeping him informed whenever you think someone has violated a rule
    C.   you're interested in improving the job by continually coming to him with suggestions
    D.   you're willing to do your share by completing assigned tasks properly and on time

4. On the rapid transit system, it would be *MOST* logical to expect to find floodlights located in   4._____

    A.   subway storage rooms
    B.   maintenance headquarters
    C.   outdoor train storage yards
    D.   under-river tunnels

5. The. most important reason for insisting on neatness in maintenance quarters is that it   5._____

    A.   keeps the men busy in slack periods
    B.   prevents tools from becoming rusty
    C.   makes a good impression on visitors and officials
    D.   decreases the chances of accidents to employees

6. Maintenance workers whose duties require them to work on the tracks in the subway generally work in pairs. The *LEAST* likely of the following possible reasons for this practice is that   6._____

    A.   some of the work requires two men
    B.   the men can help each other in case of accident

C. there is too much equipment for one man to carry
D. it protects against vandalism

7. A foreman reprimands a helper for walking across the subway tracks unnecessarily in violation of the rules and regulations. The *BEST* reaction of the helper in this situation is to

    A. tell the foreman that he was careful and that he did not take any chances
    B. explain that he took this action to save time
    C. keep quiet and accept the criticism
    D. demand that the foreman show him the rule he violated

7.____

8. The type of screwdriver which will develop the greatest turning force is a

    A. screwdriver-bit and brace
    B. spiral push-type
    C. standard straight handle
    D. straight handle with ratchet

8.____

9. The book of rules and regulations states that employees must give notice in person or by telephone of their intention to be absent from work at least one hour before they are scheduled to report for duty. The *MOST* logical reason for having this rule is so that

    A. the employee's excuse can be checked
    B. the employee's pay can be stopped for that day
    C. a substitute can be provided
    D. absences will be limited to necessary ones

9.____

10. In a shop, it would be most necessary to provide a fitted cover on the metal container for

    A. old paint brushes
    C. sand
    B. oily ragsa nd waste
    D. broken glass

10.____

11. A vertical cylindrical tank 4 feet in diameter and 5 feet high has a capacity of 470 gallons. The number of gallons in the tank when filled to a depth of 1'6" is nearest to

    A. 45   B. 95   C. 140   D. 180

11.____

12. A crate contains 3 pieces of equipment weighing 43, 59, and 66 pounds respectively. If the crate is lifted by 4 men each lifting one corner of the crate, the average number of pounds lifted by each of the men is

    A. 56   B. 51   C. 42   D. 36

12.____

13. The principal objection to using water from a hose to put out a fire involving electrical equipment is that

    A. serious shock may result
    B. metal parts may rust
    C. fuses may blow out
    D. it may spread the fire

13.____

14. Maintainers of the transit system are required to report defective equipment to their superiors, even when the maintenance of the particular equipment is handled by another bureau. The purpose of this rule is to

14.____

A. punish employees who don't do their jobs
B. have repairs made before serious trouble occurs
C. keep employees on their toes
D. reward those who keep their eyes open

15. When summoning an ambulance for an injured person, it is most important to give the   15.____

    A. name of the injured person
    B. nature of the injuries
    C. cause of the accident
    D. location of the injured person

16. Employees using supplies from one of the first aid kits available throughout the subway   16.____
are required to submit an immediate report of the occurrence. Logical reasoning shows
that the most important purpose for this report is so that the

    A. supplies used will be sure to be replaced
    B. first aid kit can be properly sealed again
    C. employee will be credited for his action
    D. record of first aid supplies will be up to date

17. The tool shown at the right is used to   17.____

    A. set nails
    B. set lead anchors
    C. drill holes in concrete
    D. centerpunch for holes

18. The tool shown at the right is a   18.____ 
    A. punch
    B. Phillips-type screwdriver
    C. drill holder
    D. socket wrench

19. The tool shown at the right is   19.____
    A. an Allen-head wrench
    B. an offset screwdriver
    C. a double scraper
    D. a nail puller

20. The tool shown at the right is   20.____
    A. an offset wrench
    B. a spanner wrench
    C. a box wrench
    D. an open end wrench

21. The tool shown at the right is used to   21.____ 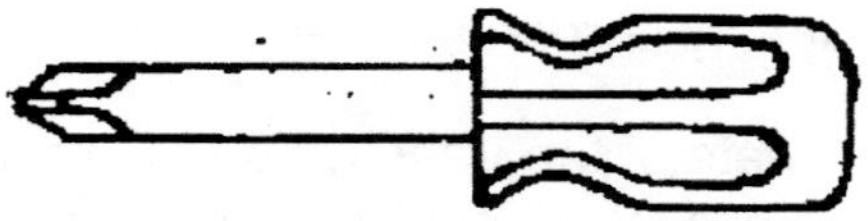
    A. ream holes in wood
    B. countersink holes in soft metals
    C. turn Phillips-head screws
    D. drill holes in concrete

22. If the head of a hammer has become loose on the handle, it should properly be tightened 22.____
by
    A. driving the handle further into the head
    B. using a slightly larger wedge
    C. driving a nail alongside the present wedge
    D. soaking the handle in water

23. The right angle shown has been divided into three parts. 23.____
The number of degrees in the unmarked part is
    A. 46
    B. 36
    C. 21
    D. 6

$33°$

$21°$

24. Assume that you have burned your hand accidentally while on the job. The POOREST 24.____
first aid remedy for the burn would be

    A. tannic acid   B. iodine
    C. vaseline   D. baking soda

25. The decimal which is nearest 33/64 is 25.____

    A. 0.516   B. 0.500   C. 34/64   D. 1.939

26. A rule of the transit system is that the telephone must not be used for personal calls. The 26.____
most important reason for this rule is that the added personal calls

    A. require additional operators
    B. waste company time
    C. tie up telephones which may be urgently needed for company business
    D. increase telephone maintenance

27. The main purpose of period inspections made by the maintainers on transit system 27.____
equipment is probably to

    A. encourage the men to take better care of the equipment
    B. discover minor faults before they develop into serious breakdowns
    C. make the men familiar with the equipment
    D. keep the maintenance men busy during otherwise slack periods

28. A maintainer puts in the following order, "standard stranded, No. 1 gage, bare, galva- 28.____
nized, high strength, steel wire." The required missing information is the

    A. length   B. diameter   C. type   D. material

29. A coil-spring one foot long has a mark 3 inches from the left end. If this spring is 29.____
stretched from one end to the other of a yardstick, the mark will be at

    A. 1" on yardstick   B. 3" on yardstick
    C. 9" on yardstick   D. 12" on yardstick

30. There is a series of holes along a straight line in a piece. The first hole is 1", the second   30.____
hole is 3/4", the 3rd is 1/2" and the 4th is 1/4". "If this pattern repeats continuously, the
10th hole is

    A. 1"   B. 3/4"   C. 1/2"   D. 1/4"

31. A rule of the transit system states that, "In walking on the track, walk opposite to the   31.____
direction of traffic on that track if possible." By logical reasoning, the principal safety idea
behind this rule is that the man on the track

    A. is more likely to see an approaching train
    B. will be seen more readily by the motorman
    C. need not be as careful
    D. is better able to judge the speed of the train

32. From your observation and knowledge of the subway, the logical reason that certain   32.____
employees who work on the tracks carry small parts in fiber pails rather than steel pails is
that fiber pails

    A. are stronger
    B. can't rust
    C. can't be dented by rough usage
    D. do not conduct electricity

33. When you are newly assigned as a helper to an experienced maintainer, he is most likely   33.____
to give you good training if your attitude is that

    A. you need the benefit of his experience
    B. he is responsible for your progress
    C. you have the basic knowledge but lack the details
    D. he should do the job where little is to be learned

34. An employee will most likely avoid accidental injury if he   34.____

    A. stops to rest frequently
    B. works alone
    C. keeps mentally alert
    D. works very slowly

35. When making a piping or conduit installation, small steel pipe is best turned by using a   35.____

    A. monkey wrench   B. stillson wrench
    C. spanner wrench   D. chain wrench

36. A box contains an equal number of iron and brass castings. Each iron casting weighs 2   36.____
pounds and each brass casting one pound. If the box contents weigh 240 lbs., the number of brass pieces in the box is

    A. 40   B. 80   C. 120   D. 160

37. The sum of 5 feet 2-3/4 inches, 8 feet 1/2 inch, and 12-1/2 inches is   37.____

    A. 25 feet 3-3/4 inches   B. 14 feet 3-3/4 inches
    C. 13 feet 5-3/4 inches   D. 13 feet 3-3/4 inches

38. It ordinarily requires 5 days for 2 men to complete a certain job. If the management wants to have this work done in two days, the number of men required would be

    38.____

   A. 10   B. 7   C. 6   D. 5

39. If your maintainer makes contact with a 600-volt conductor and remains in contact, your first action should be to

    39.____

   A. search for the disconnecting switch
   B. ground the conductor with a bare wire
   C. pull him loose by his clothing
   D. cut the conductor

40. Before using an electric drill to make a hole in a piece of scrap iron, it is best to mark the location of the hole with a center punch in order to

    40.____

   A. make the location easier to see
   B. keep the drill from wandering
   C. C . eliminate the need for a marking device
   D. keep the fuse from blowing

41. Small cuts or injuries should be

    41.____

   A. taken care of immediately to avoid infection
   B. ignored because they are seldom important
   C. ignored unless they are painful
   D. taken care of at the end of the day

42. If you feel that one of your co-workers is not doing his share of the work, your best procedure is to

    42.____

   A. increase your own output as a good example
   B. reduce your work output to bring this matter to a head
   C. point this out to the foreman
   D. take no action and continue to do your job properly

43. In case of accident, employees who witnessed the accident are required by the rules to make *INDIVIDUAL* written reports on prescribed forms as soon as possible. The most logical reason for requiring such individual reports rather than a single joint report signed by all witnesses is because the individual reports are

    43.____

   A. more likely to result in decreasing the number of accidents
   B. less likely to be lost at the same time
   C. less likely to contain unnecessary information
   D. more likely to give the complete picture

44. If a helper finds two orders on his headquarters bulletin board giving conflicting instructions with regard to his work, his most helpful action would be to

    44.____

   A. call it to the attention of his superior
   B. comply with the order which is easier to follow
   C. follow the order which is best in his judgment
   D. defer that part of the work until a clarifying order is posted

45. The purpose of giving certain transit employees training in first aid is to   45.____

    A. provide temporary emergency aid
    B. eliminate the need for calling doctors in accident cases
    C. save money
    D. decrease the number of accidents

46. When you are first appointed as a helper and are assigned to work with a maintainer, he will probably expect you to   46.____

    A. make plenty of mistakes
    B. do very little work
    C. do all of the unpleasant work
    D. pay close attention to instructions

47. According to a safety report, a frequent cause of accidents to workers is the improper use of tools. The most helpful conclusion that you can draw from this statement is that   47.____

    A. most tools are difficult to use properly
    B. most tools are dangerous to use
    C. many accidents from tools are unavoidable
    D. many accidents from tools occur because of poor working habits

48. The best way to locate a point on the floor directly below the center of a hole in the ceiling is to use a   48.____

    A. plumb bob   B. measuring tape
    C. folding rule   D. center punch

49. It is generally known that the voltage of the third rail on the New York City subway system is about   49.____

    A. 120   B. 600   C. 1000   D. 3000

50. Roadside equipment associated with rapid transit railroad operation is generally housed in a cast iron case. The case is so designed that a gasket is compressed between the door edges and the door frame when the door is locked. By logical reasoning, it is clear that the principal purpose of the gasket is to   50.____

    A. act as a cushion to prevent cracking of the cast iron
    B. seal the case so dust and water cannot enter
    C. protect the equipment in the case against vibration
    D. prevent the door from becoming sealed tight by rust

———————

KEY (CORRECT ANSWERS)

1.	C	11.	C	21.	C	31.	A	41.	A
2.	B	12.	C	22.	B	32.	D	42.	D
3.	D	13.	A	23.	B	33.	A	43.	D
4.	C	14.	B	24.	B	34.	C	44.	A
5.	D	15.	D	25.	A	35.	B	45.	A
6.	D	16.	A	26.	C	36.	B	46.	D
7.	C	17.	C	27.	B	37.	B	47.	D
8.	A	18.	D	28.	A	38.	D	48.	A
9.	C	19.	B	29.	C	39.	C	49.	B
10.	B	20.	D	30.	B	40.	B	50.	B

EXAMINATION SECTION
TEST 1

DIRECTIONS: Each question or incomplete statement is followed by several suggested answers or completions. Select the one that *BEST* answers the question or completes the statement. *PRINT THE LETTER OF THE CORRECT ANSWER IN THE SPACE AT THE RIGHT.*

1. Employees of the transit system are cautioned, as a safety measure, not to use water to extinguish fires involving electrical equipment. One logical reason for this caution is that the water

    A. may transmit electrical shock to the user
    B. may crack hot insulation
    C. will not extinguish a fire started by electricity
    D. will cause harmful steam

1.____

2. As compared with solid wire, stranded wire of the same gage size is

    A. given a higher current rating
    B. easier to skin
    C. larger in total diameter
    D. better for high voltage

2.____

3. When drilling holes in concrete from the top of an extension ladder, it is *LEAST* important to

    A. wear goggles
    B. wear gloves
    C. hook one leg through the rung of the ladder
    D. wear a helmet

3.____

4. Motor frames are usually positively grounded by a special connection in order to

    A. remove static   B. protect against lightning
    C. provide a neutral   D. protect against shock

4.____

5. If a live conductor is contacted accidentally, the severity of the electrical shock is determined primarily by

    A. the size of the conductor
    B. whether the current is a.c. or d.c.
    C. the contact resistance
    D. the current in the conductor

5.____

Items 6-15.

Items 6 through 15 in Column I are electrical equipment parts each of which is commonly made from one of the materials listed in Column II. For each part in Column I, select the most appropriate material from Column II. *PRINT,* in the correspondingly numbered item space at the right, the letter given beside your selected material.

	COLUMN I (electrical equipment parts)		COLUMN II (materials)	
6.	d.c. circuit breaker arcing-tips	A.	copper	6.____
7.	cartridge fuse casing	B.	silver	7.____
8.	pig-tail jumpers for contacts	C.	porcelain	8.____
9.	commutator bars	D.	carbon	9.____
10.	bearing oil-rings	E.	transite	10.____
11.	cores for wound heater-coils	H.	wood	11.____
12.	center contact in screw lamp-sockets	J.	lead	12.____
13.	acid storage battery terminals	K.	brass	13.____
14.	arc chutes	L.	phosphor bronze	14.____
15.	operating sticks for disconnecting switches	M.	fiber	15.____

16. One of the rules of the transit system prohibits "horseplay". For electrical employees, this rule is most important because   16.____

    A. horseplay wastes company time
    B. electrical work does not permit relaxation at any time
    C. electrical work is very complicated
    D. men are liable to injury when so engaged

17. If a snap switch rated at 5 amperes is used for an electric heater which draws 10 amperes, the most likely result is that the   17.____

    A. circuit fuse will be blown
    B. circuit wiring will become hot
    C. heater output will be halved
    D. switch contacts will become hot

18. If you are assigned by your foreman to a job which you do not understand, you should   18.____

    A. explain and request further instructions from your foreman
    B. try to do the job because you learn from experience
    C. do the job to the best of your ability as that is all that can be expected
    D. ask another foreman since your foreman should have explained the job when it was assigned

19. In carrying a length of conduit through a reasonably crowded subway station, a maintainer and his helper would follow the best procedure if   19.____

    A. the helper held one end and the maintainer the other at arm's length downward
    B. the helper carried it near the middle and the maintainer went ahead to warn passengers

C. each employee carried one end on his shoulder
D. the two employees carry at the 1/3 and 2/3 points respectively

20. To straighten a long length of wire, which has been tightly coiled, before pulling it into a 20.____
conduit run, a good method is to

    A. roll the wire into a coil in the opposite direction
    B. fasten one end to the floor and whip it against the floor from the other end
    C. draw it over a convenient edge
    D. hold the wire at one end and twist it with the pliers from the other end

21. The 110-volt bus supplying the control power in a substation is often d.c. from storage 21.____
batteries charged automatically rather than a.c. from a transformer using the a.c. main
supply. One reason is that the d.c. system

    A. requires less maintenance
    B. is more reliable
    C. requires less power
    D. permits smaller control wires

22. Mercury arc rectifiers are often used rather than rotary converters in above-ground sub- 22.____
stations in residential areas because they are

    A. cooler   B. less dangerous
    C. smaller   D. less noisy

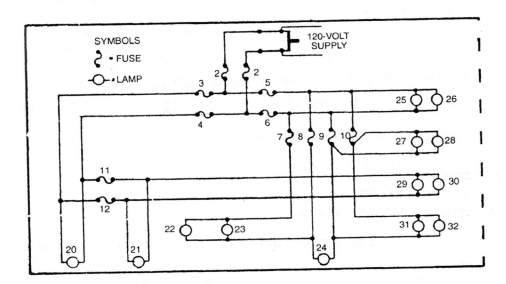

Items 23 - 31.

Items 23 through 31 are based on the above wiring diagram. All of the lamps are normally
lighted. These items in Column I are descriptions of abnormal conditions each of which is
caused by one of the faults listed in Column II. *PRINT,* in the correspondingly numbered item
space at the right, the letter given beside your selected fault.

Column I (abnormal conditions)		Column II (faults)	
23.	Lamp Nos. 24, 27, 28, 31, and 32 dark	A. Either fuse #11 or fuse #12 blown	23._
24.	Lamp Nos. 27, 28, 31, and 32 dark	B. Fuse #9 blown	24._
25.	Lamp Nos. 21, 29, and 30 dark	C. Fuse #10 blown	25._
26.	Lamp Nos. 22 and 23 dark	D. Lamp burned out	26._
27.	Only lamp No. 24 dark	E. Either fuse #9 or fuse #10 blown	27._
28.	Lamp Nos. 20, 21, 29, and 30 dark	H. Either fuse #5 or fuse #6 blown	28._
29.	Lamp Nos. 22, 23, and 24 dark	J. Fuse #8 blown	29._
		K. Fuse #7 blown	
30.	Lamp Nos. 22, 23, 24, 25, 26, 27, 28, 31, and 32 dark	L. Either fuse #3 or fuse #4 blown	30._
31.	Only lamp No. 20 dark	M. Either fuse #1 or fuse #2 blown	31._

32. The wire size most commonly used for branch circuits in residences is   32._

    A. #14   B. #16   C. #12   D. #18

33. If the applied voltage on an incandescent lamp is increased 10%, the lamp will   33._

    A. have a longer life
    B. consume less power
    C. burn more brightly
    D. fail by insulation breakdown

34. You would expect that the overload trip coil on an ordinary air circuit breaker would have   34._

    A. heavy wire   B. fine wire
    C. many turns   D. heavily insulated wire

35. A cycle counter is an electrical timer which, when energized by alternating current, counts the number of cycles until it is deenergized. If a cycle counter is energized from a 60-cycle power supply for ten seconds, the reading of the instrument should be   35._

    A. 6   B. 10   C. 60   D. 600

36. Artificial respiration should be administered to the victim of electric shock *ONLY* if he is *NOT*   36._

    A. conscious   B. bleeding
    C. breathing   D. burned

37. A rule of the transit system states that, "In walking on the track, walk opposite the direction of traffic on that track if possible". By logical reasoning, the principal safety idea behind this rule is that the man on the track

    A. is more likely to see an approaching train
    B. will be seen more readily by the motorman
    C. need not be as careful
    D. is better able to judge the speed of the train

37._____

38. The most practical way to determine in the field if a large coil of #14 wire has the required length for a given job is to

    A. weigh the coil
    B. measure one turn and count the turns
    C. unroll it into another coil
    D. make a visual comparison with a full coil

38._____

39. A frequency meter is constructed as a potential device, that is, to be connected across the line. A logical reason for this is that

    A. only the line voltage has frequency
    B. a transformer may then be used with it
    C. the reading will be independent of the varying current
    D. it is safer than a series device

39._____

40. If you feel that one of your co-workers is not doing his share of the work, your best procedure is to

    A. point this out to the foreman
    B. reduce your output to bring the matter to a head
    C. increase your own output as a good example
    D. take no action and continue to do your job properly

40._____

41. It is usually not safe to connect 110 volts d.c. to a magnet coil designed for 110 volts a.c. because the

    A. insulation is insufficient
    B. iron may overheat
    C. wire may overheat
    D. inductance may be too high

41._____

42. The most satisfactory temporary replacement for a 40-watt, 120-volt incandescent lamp, if an identical replacement is not available, is a lamp rated at

    A. 100 watts, 240 volts
    B. 60 watts, 130 volts
    C. 40 watts, 32 volts
    D. 15 watts, 120 volts

42._____

43. If the following bare copper wire sizes were arranged in the order of increasing weight per 1000 feet, the correct arrangement would be

    A. #00, #40, #8
    B. #40, #00, #8
    C. #00, #8, #40
    D. #40, #8, #00

43._____

44. The purpose of having a rheostat in the field circuit of a d.c. shunt motor is to 44.___

    A. control the speed of the motor
    B. minimize the starting current
    C. limit the field current to a safe value
    D. reduce sparking at the brushes

45. If the maintainer to whom you are assigned gives you a job to be done in a certain way 45.___
and, after starting the job, you think of another method which you are convinced is better,
you should

    A. follow the procedure given by the maintainer since he most likely would insist on
his method anyhow
    B. request his opinion of your method before proceeding further
    C. try your own method since the maintainer probably will not know the difference
    D. inform the foreman next time he comes around

46. The resistance of a 1000-ft. length of a certain size copper wire is required to be 10.0 46.___
ohms $\pm$ 2%. This wire would *NOT* be acceptable if the resistance was

    A. 10.12 ohms   B. 10.02 ohms
    C. 10.22 ohms   D. 9.82 ohms

47. The *LEAST* important action in making a good soldered connection between two wires is 47.___
to

    A. use the proper flux   B. clean the wires well
    C. use plenty of solder   D. use sufficient heat

48. When you are newly assigned as a helper to an experienced maintainer, he is most likely 48.___
to give you good training if your attitude is that

    A. he is responsible for your progress
    B. he should do the jobs where little is to be learned
    C. you need the benefit of his experience
    D. you have the basic knowledge but lack the details

49. According to the rules, electrical maintainers must not permit other employees to replace 49.___
lamps of authorized wattage with lamps of higher wattage in the working areas of such
employees. The most likely reason for this rule is

    A. to prevent such employees from injuring their eyes
    B. that higher wattage lamps cost more
    C. to avoid overloading lighting circuits
    D. to keep the cost of electricity down

50. In the subway system, it would be most logical to expect to find floodlights located in the 50.___

    A. under-river tunnels
    B. outdoor train storage yards
    C. section maintenance headquarters
    D. subway storage rooms

KEY (CORRECT ANSWERS)

1.	A	11.	C	21.	B	31.	D	41.	C
2.	C	12.	L	22.	D	32.	A	42.	B
3.	D	13.	J	23.	B	33.	C	43.	D
4.	D	14.	E	24.	C	34.	A	44.	A
5.	C	15.	H	25.	A	35.	D	45.	B
6.	D	16.	D	26.	K	36.	C	46.	C
7.	M	17.	D	27.	D	37.	A	47.	C
8.	A	18.	A	28.	L	38.	B	48.	C
9.	A	19.	A	29.	J	39.	C	49.	C
10.	K	20.	B	30.	H	40.	D	50.	B

———

TEST 2

DIRECTIONS: Each question or incomplete statement is followed by several suggested answers or completions. Select the one that *BEST* answers the question or completes the statement. *PRINT THE LETTER OF THE CORRECT ANSWER IN THE SPACE AT THE RIGHT.*

1. Of the following, the best conductor of electricity is   1.___

    A.   tungsten   B.   iron   C.   aluminum   D.   carbon

2. A 600-volt cartridge fuse is most readily distinguished from a 250-volt cartridge fuse of   2.___
the same ampere rating by comparing the

    A.   insulating materials used
    B.   shape of the ends
    C.   diameters
    D.   lengths

3. When carrying conduit, employees are cautioned against lifting with the fingers inserted   3.___
in the end. The probable reason for this caution is to avoid the possibility of

    A.   dropping and damaging the conduit
    B.   getting dirt or perspiration inside
    C.   cutting the fingers on the edge of the conduit
    D.   straining finger muscles

4. Many power-transformer cases are filled with oil. The purpose of the oil is to   4.___

    A.   prevent rusting of the core
    B.   reduce a-c hum
    C.   insulate the coils from the case
    D.   transmit heat from the coils and core case

5. In order to make certain that a 600 volt circuit is dead V. before working on it, the best   5.___
procedure is to

    A.   test with a voltmeter
    B.   "short" the circuit quickly with a piece of insulated wire
    C.   see if any of the insulated conductors are warm
    D.   disconnect one of the wires of the circuit near the feed

6. Electrical maintainers in the transit system are generally instructed in first aid in case of 6.___
electrical shock. The most likely reason for this procedure is to

    A.   decrease the number of accidents
    B.   provide temporary emergency aid
    C.   eliminate the need for calling a doctor
    D.   reduce the necessity for "killing" circuits for maintenance

7. When closing an exposed knife switch on a panel, the action should be positive and rapid   7.___
because there is less likelihood of

    A.   the operator receiving a shock
    B.   the operator being burned

    C.   the fuse blowing
    D.   injury to equipment connected to the circuit

8.   Lubrication is *NEVER* used on   8.____

    A.   a knife switch
    B.   a die when threading conduit
    C.   wires being pulled into a conduit
    D.   a commutator

9.   If one plug fuse in a 110-volt circuit blows because of a short-circuit, a 110-volt lamp   9.____
screwed into the fuse socket will

    A.   burn dimly   B.   remain dark
    C.   burn out   D.   burn normally

10.   Of the following, the *LEAST* undesirable practice if a specified wire size is not available   10.____
for part of a circuit is to

    A.   use two wires of 1/2 capacity in parallel as a substitute
    B.   use the next larger size wire
    C.   use a smaller size wire if the length is short
    D.   reduce the size of the fuse and use smaller wire

11.   If it is necessary to increase slightly the tension of an ordinary coiled spring in a relay, the   11.____
proper procedure is to

    A.   cut off one or two turns
    B.   compress it slightly
    C.   stretch it slightly
    D.   unhook one end, twist and replace

12.   The most important reason for insisting on neatness in maintenance quarters is that it   12.____

    A.   makes a good impression on visitors and officials
    B.   decreases the chances of accidents to employees
    C.   provides jobs to fill the unavoidable gaps in daily routine
    D.   prevents tools from becoming rusty

Items 13-21.

Items 13 through 21 in Column I are wiring devices each of which properly would be used at one of the locations indicated by a large dot (●) on one of the four sketches shown in Column II. For each device in Column I, select the suitable location from Column II. *PRINT,* in the correspondingly numbered item space at the right, the letter given beside your selected location.

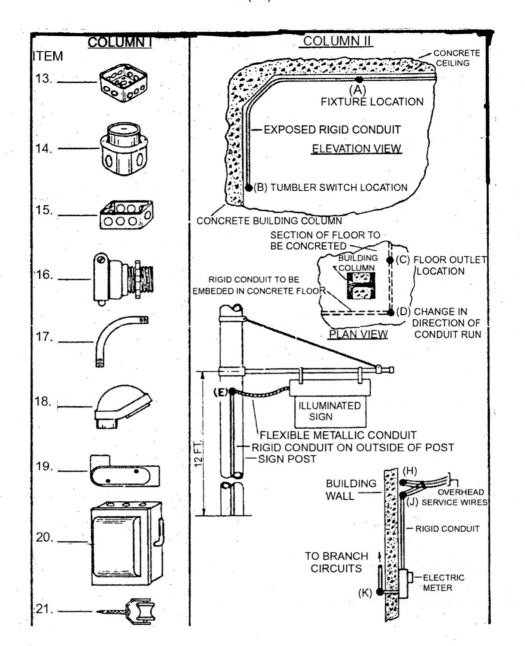

ITEM

COLUMN I

13.

14.

15.

16.

17.

18.

19.

20.

21.

COLUMN II

CONCRETE CEILING

(A) FIXTURE LOCATION

EXPOSED RIGID CONDUIT

ELEVATION VIEW

(B) TUMBLER SWITCH LOCATION

CONCRETE BUILDING COLUMN

SECTION OF FLOOR TO BE CONCRETED

BUILDING COLUMN

(C) FLOOR OUTLET LOCATION

RIGID CONDUIT TO BE EMBEDED IN CONCRETE FLOOR

(D) CHANGE IN DIRECTION OF CONDUIT RUN

PLAN VIEW

(E)

ILLUMINATED SIGN

FLEXIBLE METALLIC CONDUIT

RIGID CONDUIT ON OUTSIDE OF POST

SIGN POST

12 FT.

BUILDING WALL

(H)

OVERHEAD (J) SERVICE WIRES

RIGID CONDUIT

TO BRANCH CIRCUITS

(K)

ELECTRIC METER

13. ___

14. ___

15. ___

16. ___

17. ___

18. ___

19. ___

20. ___

21. ___

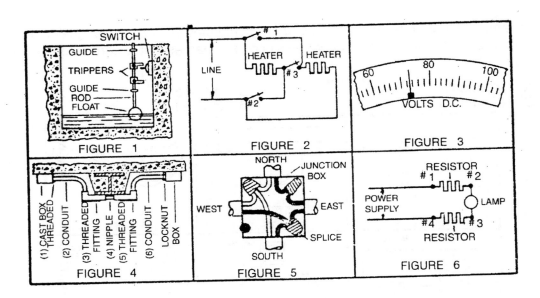

FIGURE 1
FIGURE 2
FIGURE 3
FIGURE 4
FIGURE 5
FIGURE 6

Items 22 - 27.

Items 22 through 27 refer to the figures above. Each item gives the proper figure to use with that item.

22. In Figure 1, the trippers on the float-rod operate the switch and are adjusted to start the pump motor when the water in the sump reaches a certain high level and to stop the pump when the water is down to a certain low level.
If it is decided that the pump should start sooner, the required change in tripper position on the rod is

22.____

    A.   upper tripper lowered   B.   lower tripper lowered
    C.   upper tripper raised   D.   lower tripper raised

23. In Figure 2, the greatest total amount of heat will be provided by the two heaters if

23.____

    A.   switches #2 and #3 are closed
    B.   switch #3 is closed
    C.   switches #1 and #3 are closed
    D.   switches #1, #2 and #3 are closed

24. The voltage indicated on the voltmeter scale of Figure 3 is

24.____

    A. 73.0   B. 71.5   C. 66.5   D. 60.65

25. In Figure 4, if fitting (3) is defective and must be replaced, the proper sequence of disassembly is to remove in the order given

25.____

    A.   2 then 3
    B.   4 then 3
    C.   1, 2 and 3 together; then 3
    D.   6 and 5 together; then 4 and 3

26. If the wiring in the junction box of Figure 5 is in accord with recognized good wiring practice, the power supply wires could NOT be those in the conduit going

26.____

    A.   north   B.   south   C.   east   D.   west

27. The lamp of Figure 6 is at normal brightness connected as shown. Using a third resistor, 27.___
the greatest reduction in lamp brightness occurs if that resistor is connected between
points

    A. #1 and #4   B. #1 and #2
    C. #2 and #3   D. #3 and #4

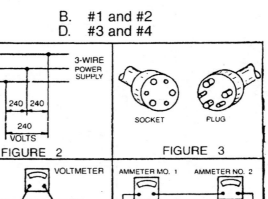

Items 28 - 33.

Items 28 through 33 refer to the figures above. Each item gives the proper figure to use with that
item.

28. In Figure 1, if the voltage of the power supply is constant, the voltage across the con- 28.___
denser is

    A. zero
    B. variable
    C. equal to the supply voltage
    D. more than the supply voltage

29. In accordance with the voltages shown in Figure 2, the power supply must be 29.___

    A. single-phase a.c.   B. two-phase a.c.
    C. three-phase a.c.   D. three-wire d.c.

30. With respect to the plug and socket in Figure 3, it is clear that the plug 30.___

    A. cannot be inserted into the socket
    B. can be inserted into the socket only one way
    C. can be inserted only two ways into the socket
    D. can be inserted three ways into the socket

31. Without knowing the battery voltage in Figure 4, it is clear that the highest current is in 31.___
the

    A. 5-ohm resistor   B. 3-ohm resistor
    C. 2-ohm resistor   D. 1-ohm resistor

32. If the three resistors in Figure 5 are of equal and relatively low resistance, the voltmeter should read   32.____

    A. one-third line voltage
    B. one-half line voltage
    C. two-thirds line voltage
    D. full line voltage

33. If the current in the circuit of Figure 6 is 6 amperes, the ammeters should read   33.____

    A. 4 amp. on meter #1 and 2 amp. on meter #2
    B. 6 amp. on each meter
    C. 2 amp. on meter #1 and 4 amp. on meter #2
    D. 3 amp. on each meter

34. The voltage drop is 24 volts across resistor   34.____

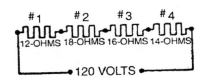

    A. #1   B. #2
    C. #3   D. #4

35. If ammeter #2 reads 60 amp., the reading of ammeter #1 should be about   35.____
    A. 4 amp.
    B. 15 amp.
    C. 60 amp.
    D. 900 amp.

36. If fuse #1 blows in the 3-wire d.c. system shown, the current in the neutral wire will   36.____
    A. increase by 1.0 amp.
    B. increase by 0.5 amp.
    C. decrease by 1.0 amp.
    D. decrease by 0.5 amp.

37. The current in the 4-ohm resistor is   37.____
    A. 5 amp.
    B. 4 amp.
    C. 3 amp.
    D. 1 amp.

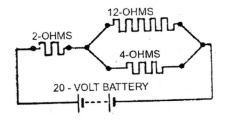

38. On the transformer, the dimension marked "X" is
    A. 9 7/8"
    B. 14"
    C. 18 1/8"
    D. 19 1/8"

38.___

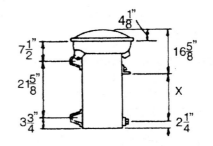

39. With the voltage drop across the four resistors as shown, the voltmeter will read
    A. 50 volts
    B. 70 volts
    C. 100 volts
    D. 170 volts

39.___

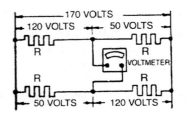

40. If each circuit originates at the switch-board, the total amount of wire required for the conduit runs shown (neglecting connections) is
    A. 5300 ft.
    B. 2650 ft.
    C. 2400 ft.
    D. 1600 ft.

40.___

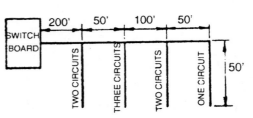

NOTE: TWO WIRES PER CIRCUIT

41. If the permissible current is 1,000 amperes for each square inch of cross section, the bus bar shown can carry
    A. 2250 amp.
    B. 2000 amp.
    C. 1750 amp.
    D. 1500 amp.

41.___

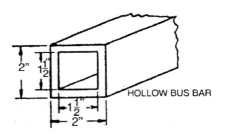

42. If the slider connecting both resistors is 9 inches from the left-hand end of the resistors, the resistance between terminals #1 and #2 is
    A. 1125 ohms
    B. 875 ohms
    C. 750 ohms
    D. 625 ohms

42.___

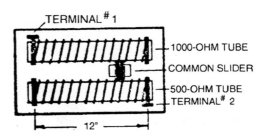

43. If the voltmeter reads 80 volts, the current in the 11-ohm resistor is
    A. 10 amp.
    B. 6.3 amp.
    C. 12 amp.
    D. 8.3 amp.

43.___

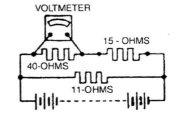

74

Questions 44 - 50.

Questions 44 through 50 show common electrical jobs. Each item shows four methods (A), (B), (C), and (D) of doing the particular job. Only *ONE* of the four methods is entirely *CORRECT* in accordance with good practice. For each item, examine the four sketches and select the sketch showing the correct method. *PRINT,* in the correspondingly numbered item space at the right, the letter given below your selected sketch.

44.

45.

46.

47.

48.

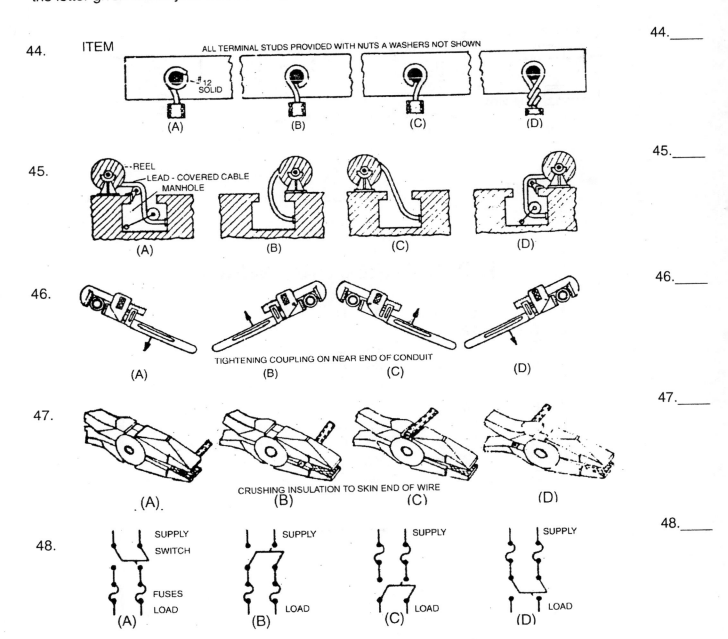

44._____

45._____

46._____

47._____

48._____

49.

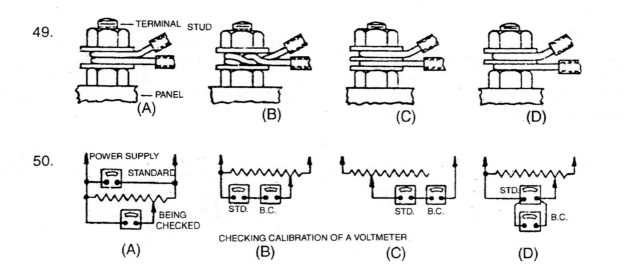

(A)   (B)   (C)   (D)

50.

CHECKING CALIBRATION OF A VOLTMETER

(A)   (B)   (C)   (D)

KEY (CORRECT ANSWERS)

1.	C	11.	A	21.	H	31.	B	41.	C
2.	D	12.	B	22.	D	32.	A	42.	B
3.	C	13.	A	23.	C	33.	B	43.	A
4.	D	14.	C	24.	A	34.	A	44.	B
5.	A	15.	B	25.	D	35.	A	45.	B
6.	B	16.	E	26.	C	36.	B	46.	A
7.	B	17.	D	27.	C	37.	C	47.	D
8.	D	18.	J	28.	C	38.	C	48.	B
9.	D	19.	E	29.	C	39.	B	49.	C
10.	B	20.	K	30.	D	40.	A	50.	D

EXAMINATION SECTION
TEST 1

DIRECTIONS: Each question or incomplete statement is followed by several suggested answers or completions. Select the one that BEST answers the question or completes the statement. *PRINT THE LETTER OF THE CORRECT ANSWER IN THE SPACE AT THE RIGHT.*

1. Motor speeds are *generally* measured directly in RPM by the use of a   1._____

    A. potentiometer   B. manometer
    C. dynamometer   D. tachometer

2. Asbestos is used as a wire covering *mainly* for protection against   2._____

    A. humidity   B. vibration   C. corrosion   D. heat

3. Assume that you were asked to get the tools for a maintainer to use in taking down a run   3._____
of exposed conduit (including outlet boxes) from its installed location on the surface of a concrete wall. The combination of tools which would *probably* prove MOST useful would be

    A. Stillson wrenches, a box wrench, and a hacksaw
    B. hacksaw, a screw driver, and an adjustable open-end wrench
    C. screw driver, a hammer, and a box wrench
    D. screw driver, an adjustable open-end wrench, and Stillson wrenches

4. Locknuts are frequently used in making electrical connections on terminal boards.   4._____
The purpose of the locknuts is to

    A. eliminate the use of flat washers
    B. prevent unauthorized personnel from tampering with the connections
    C. keep the connections from loosening through vibration
    D. increase the contact area at the connection point

5. The fasteners used to mount a cast iron box on a hollow tile wall are   5._____

    A. machine screws   B. lag screws
    C. toggle bolts   D. steel cut nails

6. The *primary* purpose of galvanizing steel conduit is to   6._____

    A. increase mechanical strength
    B. retard rusting
    C. provide a good surface for painting
    D. provide good electrical contact for grounding

7. The BEST immediate first aid if electrolyte splashes into the eyes when filling a storage   7._____
battery is to

    A. bandage the eyes to keep out light
    B. wipe the eyes dry with a soft towel
    C. induce tears to flow by staring at a bright light
    D. bathe the eyes with plenty of clean water

8. Transit workers are advised to report injuries caused by nails, no matter how slight. 8.___
The MOST important reason for this rule is that this type of injury

    A. is caused by violating safety rules
    B. can only be caused by carelessness
    C. generally causes dangerous bleeding
    D. may result in a serious condition

9. The MOST important reason for using a fuse-puller when removing a cartridge fuse from 9.___
the fuse clips is to

    A. prevent blowing of the fuse
    B. prevent injury to the fuse element
    C. reduce the chances of personal injury
    D. reduce arcing at the fuse clips

10. The *three* elements of a transistor are 10.___

    A. collector, base, emitter   B. collector, grid, cathode
    C. plate, grid, emitter   D. plate, base, cathode

11. The abbreviation D.P.D.T. used in electrical work describes a type of 11.___

    A. switch   B. motor   C. fuse   D. generator

12. The device used to change a.c. to d.c. is a 12.___

    A. frequency changer   B. regulator
    C. transformer   D. rectifier

13. The core of an electro-magnet is *usually* made of 13.___

    A. lead   B. iron   C. brass   D. aluminium

14. The application of lubricating oil to parts of electrical contacts is *generally* considered 14.___
POOR practice.
The MAIN reason for this is that the

    A. contacts will slip too much
    B. oil would cause poor electrical contact
    C. oil would reduce the contact resistance
    D. oil would cause a fire

15. Nichrome wire would be MOST suitable for use in 15.___

    A. a transformer   B. a motor
    C. a heating element   D. an incandescent lamp

16. To smooth out the ripples present in rectified a.c., the device *commonly* used is a 16.___

    A. filter   B. relay   C. spark gap   D. booster

17. One DISADVANTAGE of porcelain as an insulator is that it is 17.___

    A. only good for low voltage
    B. not satisfactory on a.c. circuits
    C. a brittle material
    D. difficult to clean

18. The gage used to determine the size of wire is called

    A. AWG   B. NPT   C. PILC   D. RHW

18.____

19. A stranded wire is given the same size designation as a solid wire if it has the same

    A. cross-sectional area   B. weight per foot
    C. overall diameter   D. strength

19.____

20. The normal voltage of the electrical circuits in most homes and offices in this area is 120. The *difference* between the maximum power that can be supplied by a 20-ampere circuit and the maximum that can be supplied by a 15-ampere circuit is

    A. 4200 watts   B. 2400 watts   C. 1800 watts   D. 600 watts

20.____

21. The term which is NOT applicable in describing the construction of a microphone is

    A. dynamic   B. carbon   C. crystal   D. feedback

21.____

22. The magnetic material used in making the high-strength permanent magnets which are now readily available, is *commonly* known as

    A. alnico   B. chromaloy   C. nichrome   D. advance

22.____

23. If a two wire circuit has a drop of 2 volts in each wire to the load and a supply voltage of 100 volts, the voltage at the load is _____ volts.

    A. 104   B. 102   C. 98   D. 96

23.____

24. A milliampere is _____ amperes.

    A. 1000   B. 100   C. .01   D. .001

24.____

25. A megohm is _____ ohms.

    A. 10   B. 100   C. 1000   D. 1,000,000

25.____

26. A circular mil is a measure of electrical conductor

    A. length   B. area   C. volume   D. weight

26.____

27. A standard pipe thread differs from a standard screw thread in that the pipe thread

    A. is tapered
    B. is deeper
    C. requires no lubrication when cutting
    D. has the same pitch for any diameter of pipe

27.____

28. The rating term "1000 ohms, 10 watts" would *generally* be applied to a

    A. heater   B. relay   C. resistor   D. transformer

28.____

29. The term "60 cycle" as applied to alternating current means

    A. one cycle in 60 seconds   B. 60 cycles per second
    C. 60 cycles per minute   D. one cycle in 60 minutes

29.____

30. The dimensions of the concrete base shown below are

    A. 12" x 20"   B. 19" x 25"   C. 21" x 27"   D. 24" x 29"

30.____

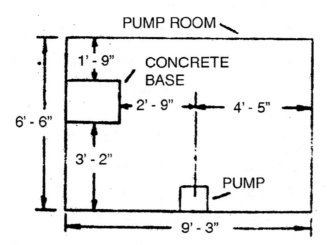

PUMP ROOM

31. Two separate adjacent lamp bulbs are placed behind each colored lens of the train signals alongside the tracks in the subway.
The *logical* reason why two bulbs are used instead of one bulb is to

    A. permit lower line voltage
    B. increase the light intensity
    C. permit the use of smaller bulbs
    D. keep the signal lighted in case one bulb fails

31.___

32. The action of a common plug fuse depends on the principle that the

    A. current develops heat
    B. voltage breaks down a thin mica disk
    C. current expands and bends a link
    D. voltage develops heat

32.___

33. The load side is *usually* wired to the blades of a knife switch to

    A. prevent arcing when switch is opened
    B. make the blades dead when switch is open
    C. allow changing of fuses without opening switch
    D. prevent blowing fuse when opening switch

33.___

34. Two 500-watt lamps connected in series across a 110-volt line draw 2 amperes.
The *total* power consumed is _____ watts.

    A. 1,000   B. 250   C. 220   D. 55

34.___

35. Before connecting two generators in parallel to a common bus they should ALWAYS have the same

    A. voltage   B. capacity   C. resistance   D. speed

35.___

36. Certain electrical control circuits in power stations must be kept energized at all times even in case of complete station shut down.
Based on this fact, the BEST source of power supply for these circuit is from

    A. the main generator   B. a motor-generator set
    C. a rectifier   D. a storage battery

36.___

37. Electrical helpers on the subway system are instructed in the use of fire extinguishers. The *probable* reason for including helpers in this instruction is that the helper

    A. cannot do the more important work
    B. may be the cause of a fire because of his inexperience
    C. may be alone when a fire starts
    D. will become interested in fire prevention

37._____

38. If a 100-watt tungsten lamp is compared with a 25-watt tungsten lamp of the same voltage rating, the resistance of the 100-watt lamp is

    A. higher
    B. lower
    C. the same
    D. higher with A.C., lower with D.C.

38._____

39. If a low resistance is connected in parallel with a higher resistance, the combined resistance is

    A. ALWAYS *less* than the low resistance
    B. ALWAYS *more* than the high resistance
    C. ALWAYS between the values of the high and the low resistance
    D. *higher* or *lower* than the low resistance depending on the value of the higher resistance

39._____

40. Connecting dry cells in parallel instead of in series

    A. *increases* the current capacity of the battery
    B. *decreases* the current capacity of the battery
    C. *increases* the battery voltage
    D. *decreases* the life of the battery

40._____

___

KEY (CORRECT ANSWERS)

1. D	11. A	21. D	31. D
2. D	12. D	22. A	32. A
3. D	13. B	23. D	33. B
4. C	14. B	24. D	34. C
5. C	15. C	25. D	35. A
6. B	16. A	26. B	36. D
7. D	17. C	27. A	37. C
8. D	18. A	28. C	38. B
9. C	19. A	29. B	39. A
10. A	20. D	30. B	40. A

TEST 2

DIRECTIONS: Each question or incomplete statement is followed by several suggested answers or completions. Select the one that BEST answers the question or completes the statement. *PRINT THE LETTER OF THE CORRECT ANSWER IN THE SPACE AT THE RIGHT.*

1. Maintainers of the transit system are required to report defective equipment to their superiors, even when the maintenance of the particular equipment is handled entirely by another bureau.
The purpose of this rule is to

    A. fix responsibility   B. discourage slackers
    C. encourage alertness   D. prevent accidents

1.___

2. To determine which wire of a two-wire 120-volt a.c. line is the underground wire, the BEST procedure is to

    A. obtain the polarity by connecting a voltmeter across the line
    B. quickly ground each line in turn
    C. connect one lead of a test lamp to the conduit; and test with the other
    D. test with the fingers to ground

2.___

3. Condensers are often connected across relay contacts that make and break frequently. The purpose of using condensers in this manner is to

    A. store a charge for the next operation
    B. reduce pitting of the contacts
    C. balance the inductance of the circuit
    D. make the relay slow acting

3.___

4. A conductor used as a ground wire is *usually*

    A. insulated   B. clamped to the metallic ground
    C. fused   D. #14 A.W.G.

4.___

5. If fuse clips become hot under normal circuit load, the MOST probable cause is that the fuse

    A. rating is too low   B. rating is too high
    C. clips are too loose   D. clips are too tight

5.___

6. The liquid in a lead-acid storage battery is called the

    A. anode   B. cathode
    C. electrolyte   D. electrode

6.___

7. In carrying a length of conduit through a reasonably crowded subway station, a maintainer and his helper would follow the BEST procedure if

    A. the helper held one end and the maintainer the other at arm's length downward
    B. the helper carried it near the middle and the maintainer went ahead to warn passengers
    C. each employee carried one end on his shoulder
    D. the two employees carry at the 1/3 and 2/3 points respectively

7.___

8. As a helper you are assigned to work with a maintainer. During the course of the work, you realize that the maintainer is about to violate a basic safety rule.
   In this case the BEST thing for you to do is to

   A. walk away from him so that you will not become involved
   B. say nothing until he actually violates this rule and then call it to his attention
   C. immediately call it to his attention
   D. say nothing, but later report this action to the foreman

   8._____

9. A rule of the transit system is that the system telephones must NOT be used for personal calls.
   The MOST important reason for this rule is that such personal calls

   A. increase telephone maintenance
   B. tie up telephones which may be urgently needed for company business
   C. waste company time
   D. require additional operators

   9._____

10. Commutators are found on

    A. mercury rectifiers
    C. circuit breakers
    B. D.C. motors
    D. alternators

    10._____

11. A 200 R.P.M. motor has its centrifugal speed switch set to open at 110% speed.
    The switch will open at _____ R.P.M.

    A. 310   B. 220   C. 110   D. 10

    11._____

12. A 2-ohm resistor and a 1-ohm resistor connected in parallel2 take a total current of 30 amperes.
    The current in the 1-ohm resistor is _____ amperes.

    A. 10   B. 15   C. 20   D. 30

    12._____

13. The device *commonly* used to measure the insulation resistance of a transformer winding is

    A. an ammeter
    C. a wattmeter
    B. a megger
    D. a Wheatstone bridge

    13._____

14. A D.C. wattmeter has

    A. a voltage coil and a current coil
    B. two current coils
    C. two voltage coils
    D. three current coils

    14._____

15. A 10-24 machine screw necessarily differs from a 12-24 machine screw in

    A. diameter
    C. length
    B. threads per inch
    D. shape of head

    15._____

16. A power transformer with a ratio of 2 to 1 is fully loaded with 1,000 watts on the secondary.
    It is reasonable to expect a primary input of _____ watts.

    A. 500   B. 990   C. 1010   D. 2000

    16._____

17. The helper who would probably be rated *highest* by his supervisor is the one who   17.___

    A. makes many suggestions on work procedures
    B. never lets the maintainer do heavy lifting
    C. asks many questions about the work
    D. listens to instructions and carries them out

18. A "shunt" is used in parallel with a meter measuring high currents to   18.___

    A. increase the meter resistance
    B. protect the meter against short circuits
    C. reduce the meter current
    D. steady the meter needle

19. A transit employee is required to make a written report of any unusual occurrences promptly.   19.___
The BEST reason for requiring such promptness is that

    A. the report will tend to be more accurate as to facts
    B. the employee will not be as likely to forget to make the report
    C. there is always a tendency to do a better job under pressure
    D. the report may be too long if made at an employee's convenience

20. One thousand volts d.c. is to be tried out on the third-rail of an experimental section of a rapid-transit railroad to be built for another city. This voltage is higher than the third-rail voltage of the New York City subways by about _____ volts.   20.___

    A. 100   B. 200   C. 300   D. 400

21. The terminal voltage with batteries connected as shown is _____ volts.   21.___
    A. 0
    B. 1 1/2
    C. 3
    D. 6

TERMINAL VOLTAGE

4 CELLS EACH OF 1 1/2 VOLTS

22. The voltage across terminal 1 and terminal 2 of the transformer connected as shown is _____ volts.   22.___
    A. 50
    B. 100
    C. 200
    D. 400

TERM 1

50 - TURNS 50 - TURNS TERM 2
100 - TURNS
100 VOLTS

23. The total resistance in the circuit shown between terminal 1 and terminal 2 is _____ ohms.   23.___
    A. 1 1/2
    B. 6
    C. 9
    D. 15

6 - OHMS
5 - OHMS
6 - OHMS
TERM 1
TERM 2

24. The power used by the heater shown is
_____ watts.
   A. 120
   B. 720
   C. 2400
   D. 4320

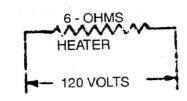

25. The current flowing through the 6-ohm resistor in the circuit shown is _____ amperes.
   A. 1
   B. 3
   C. 6
   D. 11

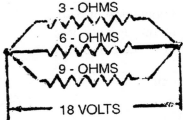

26. The voltage across the 30-ohm resistor in the circuit shown is _____ volts.
   A. 4
   B. 20
   C. 60
   D. 120

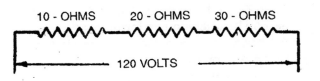

27. The current in the wire at the point indicated by the arrow is _____ amperes.

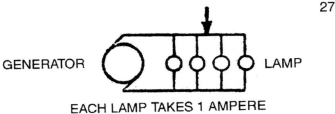

28. The sketch shows a head-on view of a three-pronged plug used with portable electrical power tools. Considering the danger of shock when using such tools, it is evident that the function of the U-shaped prong is to
   A. insure that the other two prongs enter the outlet with the proper polarity
   B. provide a half-voltage connection when doing light work
   C. prevent accidental pulling of the plug from the outlet
   D. connect the metallic shell of the tool motor to ground

28

29. The reading of the ammeter should be
    A. 4.0
    B. 2.0
    C. 1.0
    D. .05

29.____

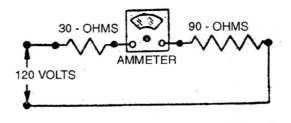

30. Applying your knowledge of electrical measuring instruments, it is *most likely* that the scale shown is for
    A. an ohmmeter
    B. a voltmeter
    C. an ammeter
    D. a wattmeter

30.____

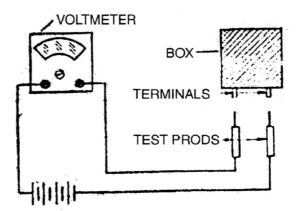

31. Assume that you have decided to test a sealed box having two terminals by using the hook-up shown. When you hold the test prods on the terminals, the voltmeter needle swings upscale and then quickly returns to zero. As an initial conclusion you would be CORRECT in assuming that the box contained a
    A. condenser
    B. choke
    C. rectifier
    D. resistor

31.____

32. If each of the four 90° conduit elbows has the dimensions shown, the distance S is
    A. 20"
    B. 22"
    C. 24"
    D. 26"

32.____

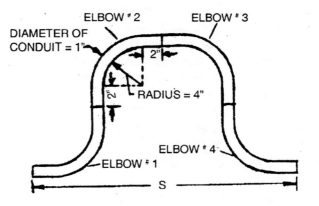

33. The purpose of the auxiliary blade on the knife switch shown is to
    A. delay the opening of the circuit when the handle is pulled open
    B. cut down arcing by opening the circuit quickly
    C. retain the blades in place
    D. increase the capacity of the switch

33.____

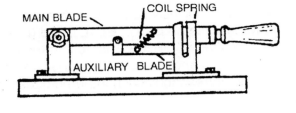

34. The sketch shows the four resistance dials and the multiplying dial of a resistance bridge. The four resistance dials can be set to any value of resistance up to 10,000 ohms, and the multiplier can be set at any of the nine points shown. In their present positions, the five pointers indicate a reading of
    A. 13.60
    B. 136.000
    C. 131.600
    D. 13.16

34.____

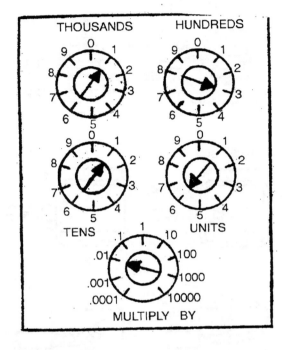

35. Regardless of the battery voltage, it is clear that the SMALLEST current is in the resistor having a resistance of
    A. 200 ohms
    B. 300 ohms
    C. 400 ohms
    D. 500 ohms

35.____

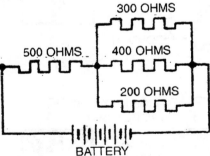

36. The five lamps shown are each rated at 120-volts, 60-watts. If all are good lamps, lamp no. 5 will be
    A. much brighter than normal
    B. about its normal brightness
    C. much dimmer than normal
    D. completely dark

36.____

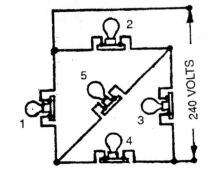

87

QUESTIONS 37-40.

Questions 37-40 inclusive show common electrical maintenance installation jobs. Each question shows four methods (A), (B), (C), and (D) of doing the particular job. Only ONE of the four methods is entirely CORRECT in accordance with good practice. For each question, examine the four sketches and select the sketch showing the correct method. PRINT on your answer sheet, in the correspondingly numbered question space, the letter given below your selected sketch.

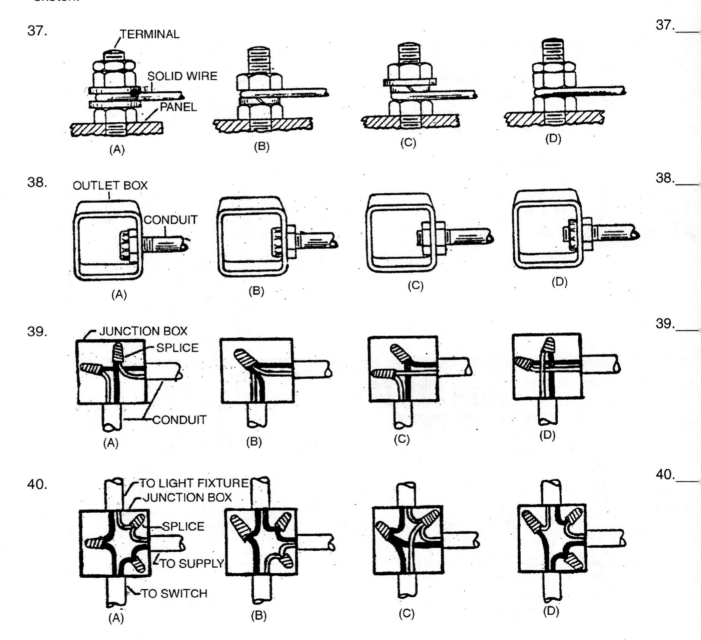

37.

37.____

38.

38.____

39.

39.____

40.

40.____

KEY (CORRECT ANSWERS)

1.	D	11.	B	21.	C	31.	A
2.	C	12.	C	22.	A	32.	D
3.	B	13.	B	23.	B	33.	B
4.	B	14.	A	24.	C	34.	D
5.	C	15.	A	25.	B	35.	C
6.	C	16.	C	26.	C	36.	D
7.	A	17.	D	27.	B	37.	A
8.	C	18.	C	28.	D	38.	B
9.	B	19.	A	29.	C	39.	C
10.	B	20.	D	30.	A	40.	A

EXAMINATION SECTION
TEST 1

DIRECTIONS: Each question or incomplete statement is followed by several suggested answers or completions. Select the one that *BEST* answers the question or completes the statement. *PRINT THE LETTER OF THE CORRECT ANSWER IN THE SPACE AT THE RIGHT.*

1. Of the following, the best conductor of electricity is   1.____

    A. aluminum   B. carbon
    C. copper   D. water

2. Good practice requires that the end of a piece of conduit be reamed after it has been cut   2.____
to length. The purpose of the reaming is to

    A. prevent insulation damage when pulling in the wires
    B. finish the conduit accurately to length
    C. make the threading easier
    D. remove loose rust

3. According to the national electrical code, a run of conduit between two outlet boxes   3.____
should not contain more than four quarter-bends. The most likely reason for this limita-
tion is that more bends will

    A. result in cracking the conduit
    B. make the pulling of the wire too difficult
    C. increase the wire length unnecessarily
    D. not be possible in one standard length of conduit

4. Asbestos is commonly used as the covering of electric wires in locations where there is   4.____
likely to be high

    A. voltage   B. temperature
    C. humidity   D. current

5. The *LEAST* likely result of a severe electric shock is   5.____

    A. unconsciousness   B. a burn
    C. stoppage of breathing   D. bleeding

6. Electrical helpers on the subway system are instructed in the use of fire extinguishers.   6.____
The probable reason for including helpers in this instruction is that the helper

    A. cannot do the more important work
    B. may be the cause of a fire because of his inexperience
    C. may be alone when a fire starts
    D. will become interested in fire prevention

7. Transit employees are cautioned, as a safety measure, not to use water to extinguish   7.____
fires involving electrical equipment. One logical reason for this caution is that the water

    A. will cause harmful steam
    B. will not extinguish a fire started by electricity

C. may transmit electrical shock to the user
D. may crack hot insulators

8. When the level of the liquid in a lead-acid storage cell is low, a maintainer should normally add   8.___

    A. alkaline solution   B. diluted alcohol
    C. battery acid   D. distilled water

9. Portable lamp cord is likely to have   9.___

    A. steel armor   B. stranded wires
    C. paper insulation   D. number 8 wire

10. The one of the following terms which could *NOT* correctly be used in describing a knife switch is   10.___

    A. quick-break   B. single throw
    C. four-pole   D. toggle

11. A transit employee is required to make a written report of any unusual occurrence promptly. The best reason for requiring such promptness is that   11.___

    A. the report will tend to be more accurate as to facts
    B. the employee will not be as likely to forget to make the report
    C. there is always a tendency to do a better job under pressure
    D. the report may be too long if made at an employee's convenience

12. With respect to common electric light bulbs, it is correct to state that the   12.___

    A. circuit voltage has no effect on the life of the bulb
    B. filament is made of carbon
    C. base has a left hand thread
    D. lower wattage bulb has the higher resistance

13. It is generally known that the voltage of the third rail on the New York City Transit System is about   13.___

    A. 3000   B. 1000   C. 600   D. 120

14. The resistance of a 1000-foot coil of a certain size copper wire is 10 ohms. If 300 feet is cut off, the resistance of the remainder of the coil is   14.___

    A. 7 ohms   B. 3 ohms   C. 0.7 ohms   D. 0.3 ohm

15. The term "15-ampere" is commonly used in Identifying   15.___

    A. an insulator   B. a fuse
    C. a conduit   D. an outlet box

16. When you are first appointed as a helper and are assigned to work with a maintainer, he will probably expect you to   16.___

    A. do very little work
    B. make plenty of mistakes
    C. pay close attention to instructions
    D. do all of the unpleasant work

17. When connecting the two lead wires of a test instrument to a live d.c. circuit, the best procedure is to first make the negative or ground connection and then the positive connection. The reason for this procedure is that   17.____

    A. electricity flows from positive to negative
    B. there is less danger of accidental shock
    C. the reverse procedure may blow the fuse
    D. less arcing will occur when the connection is made

Questions 18 - 24.

Questions 18 through 24 in Column I are materials each of which is commonly used for one of the electrical equipment parts listed in Column II. For each material in Column I, select the most closely associated part from Column II. *PRINT,* in the correspondingly numbered item space at the right, the letter given beside your selected part.

COLUMN I (materials)	COLUMN II (electrical equipment parts)	
18. steel	A. acid storage battery plates	18.____
19. lead	B. transformer cores	19.____
20. mica	C. d.c. motor brushes	20.____
21. porcelain	D. insulating tape	21.____
22. rubber	E. cartridge fuse cases	22.____
23. copper	H. commutator insulation	23.____
24. carbon	J. strain insulators	24.____
	K. knife-switch blades	

25. To make a good soldered connection between two stranded wires, it is *LEAST* important to   25.____

    A. twist the wires together before soldering
    B. use enough heat to make the solder flow freely
    C. clean the wires carefully
    D. apply solder to each strand before twisting the two wires together

26. When a step-up transformer is used, it increases the   26.____

    A. voltage   B. current
    C. power   D. frequency

27. Lock nuts are frequently used in making electrical connections on terminal boards. The purpose of such lock nuts is to   27.____

    A. make tighter connections with less effort
    B. make it difficult to tamper with the connections
    C. avoid stripping the threads
    D. keep the connections from loosening through vibration

28. If a fellow worker has stopped breathing after an electric shock, the best first-aid treatment is 28.___

    A. massage his chest
    B. a hot drink
    C. an application of cold compresses
    D. artificial respiration

29. According to a recent safety report, an outstanding cause of accidents to workers is the improper use of tools. The most helpful conclusion that you can draw from this statement is that 29.___

    A. most tools are dangerous to use
    B. most tools are difficult to use properly
    C. many accidents from tools occur because of poor working habits
    D. many accidents from tools are unavoidable

Questions 30 - 39.

Questions 30 through 39 refer to the use of tools shown on the next page. Read the item, and for the operation given, select the proper tool to be used from those shown. *PRINT*, in the correspondingly numbered item space at the right, the letter given below your selected tool.

30. Tightening a coupling on a piece of one-inch conduit. 30.___

31. Drilling a hole in a concrete wall for a lead anchor. 31.___

32. Bending a piece of 3/4-inch conduit. 32.___

33. Tightening a wire on the terminal of a standard electric light socket. 33.___

34. Cutting off a piece of 4/0 insulated copper cable. 34.___

35. Measuring the length of a proposed long conduit run. 35.___

36. Tightening a small nut on a terminal board. 36.___

37. Removing the burrs from the end of a piece of conduit after cutting. 37.___

38. Removing the flat rubber gasket stuck to the cover of a watertight pull box. 38.___

39. Knocking the head off a bolt that is rusted in place. 39.___

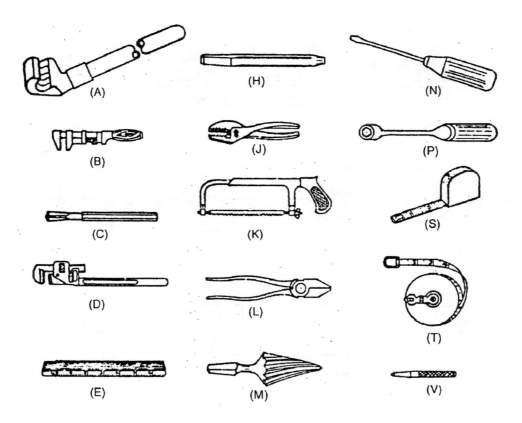

(A)   (H)   (N)

(B)   (J)   (P)

(C)   (K)   (S)

(D)   (L)   (T)

(E)   (M)   (V)

Questions 40 - 45.

Questions 40 through 45 show common electrical jobs. Each item shows four methods (A), (B), (C), and (D) of doing the particular job. Only *ONE* of the four methods is entirely *CORRECT* in accordance with good practice. For each item, examine the four sketches and select the sketch showing the correct method. *PRINT,* in the correspondingly numbered item space at the right, the letter given below your selected sketch.

40.   ITEM

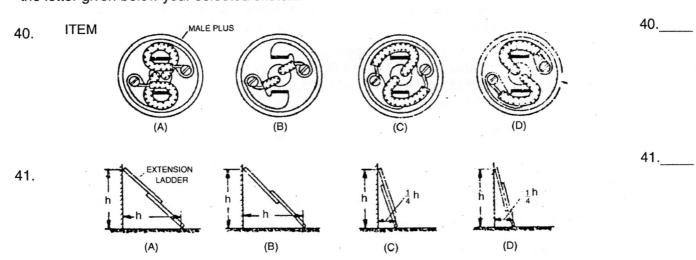

40. _____

(A)   (B)   (C)   (D)

41. _____

41.

(A)   (B)   (C)   (D)

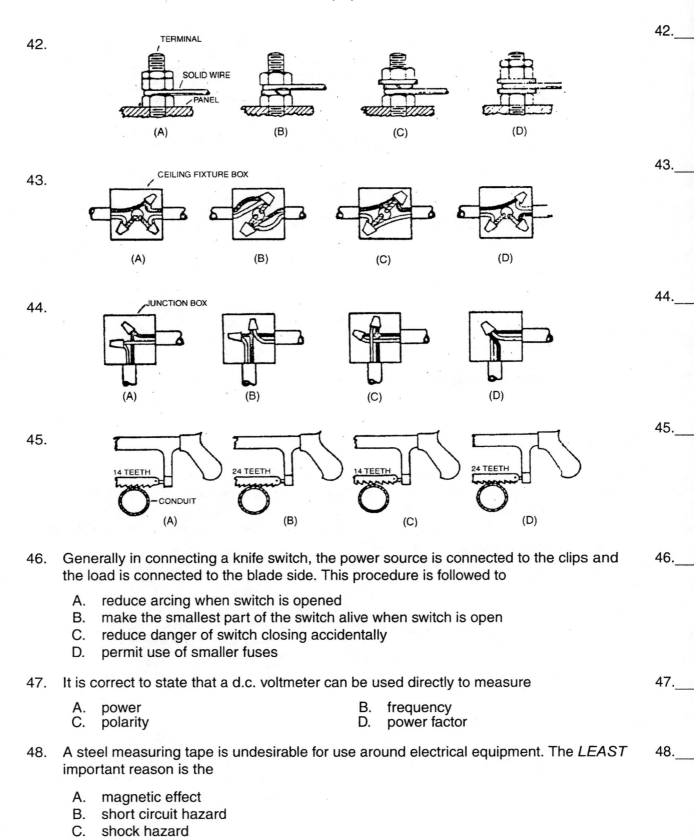

42.

43.

44.

45.

46. Generally in connecting a knife switch, the power source is connected to the clips and the load is connected to the blade side. This procedure is followed to

    A. reduce arcing when switch is opened
    B. make the smallest part of the switch alive when switch is open
    C. reduce danger of switch closing accidentally
    D. permit use of smaller fuses

46.___

47. It is correct to state that a d.c. voltmeter can be used directly to measure

    A. power   B. frequency
    C. polarity   D. power factor

47.___

48. A steel measuring tape is undesirable for use around electrical equipment. The *LEAST* important reason is the

    A. magnetic effect
    B. short circuit hazard
    C. shock hazard
    D. danger of entanglement in rotating machines

48.___

49. If you had to telephone for an ambulance because of an accident, the most important information for you to give the person who answered the telephone would be the   49._____

    A. exact time of the accident
    B. place where the ambulance is needed
    C. cause of the accident
    D. names and addresses of those injured

50. The book of rules and regulations states that employees must give notice in person or by telephone of their intention to be absent from work at least two hours before they are scheduled to report for duty. The most logical reason for having this rule is that   50._____

    A. it allows time to check the employee's excuse
    B. it has a nuisance value in limiting absences
    C. the employee's time record can be corrected in advance
    D. a substitute can be provided

KEY (CORRECT ANSWERS)

1. C	11. A	21. J	31. C	41. C
2. A	12. D	22. D	32. A	42. D
3. B	13. C	23. K	33. N	43. C
4. B	14. A	24. C	34. K	44. A
5. D	15. B	25. D	35. T	45. B
6. C	16. C	26. A	36. P	46. B
7. C	17. B	27. D	37. M	47. C
8. D	18. B	28. D	38. N	48. A
9. B	19. A	29. C	39. H	49. B
10. D	20. H	30. D	40. D	50. D

TEST 2

DIRECTIONS: Each question or incomplete statement is followed by several suggested answers or completions. Select the one that *BEST* answers the question or completes the statement. *PRINT THE LETTER OF THE CORRECT ANSWER IN THE SPACE AT THE RIGHT.*

Questions 1-7.

Questions 1 through 7 are based on the fuse information given below. Read this information carefully before answering these items.

FUSE INFORMATION

Badly bent or distorted fuse clips cannot be permitted. Sometimes the distortion or bending is so slight that it escapes notice, yet it may be the cause for fuse failures through the heat that is developed by the poor contact. Occasionally the proper spring tension of the fuse clips has been destroyed by overheating from loose wire connections to the clips. Proper contact surfaces must be maintained to avoid faulty operation of the fuse. Maintenance men should remove oxides that form on the copper and brass contacts, check the clip pressure, and make sure that contact surfaces are not deformed or bent in any way. When removing oxides, use a well-worn file and remove only the oxide film. Do not use sandpaper or emery cloth as hard particles may come off and become embedded in the contact surfaces. All wire connections to the fuse holders should be carefully inspected to see that they are tight.

1.   Fuse failure because of poor clip contact or loose connections is due to the resulting   1.___

    A.   excessive voltage   B.   increased current
    C.   lowered resistance   D.   heating effect

2.   Oxides should be removed from fuse contacts by using   2.___

    A.   a dull file   B.   emery cloth
    C.   fine sandpaper   D.   a sharp file

3.   One result of loose wire connections at the terminal of a fuse clip is stated in the above paragraph to be   3.___

    A.   loss of tension in the wire
    B.   welding of the fuse to the clip
    C.   distortion of the clip
    D.   loss of tension of the clip

4.   Simple reasoning will show that the oxide film referred to is undesirable chiefly because it   4.___

    A.   looks dull
    B.   makes removal of the fuse difficult
    C.   weakens the clips
    D.   introduces undesirable resistance

5.   Fuse clips that are bent very slightly   5.___

    A.   should be replaced with new clips
    B.   should be carefully filed

C. may result in blowing of the fuse
D. may prevent the fuse from blowing

6. Prom the fuse information paragraph it would be reasonable to conclude that fuse clips   6._____

   A. are difficult to maintain
   B. must be given proper maintenance
   C. require more attention than other electrical equipment
   D. are unreliable

7. A safe practical way of checking the tightness of the wire connection to the fuse clips of a   7._____
   live 120-volt lighting circuit is to

   A. feel the connection with your hand to see if it is warm
   B. try tightening with an insulated screwdriver or socket wrench
   C. see if the circuit works
   D. measure the resistance with an ohmmeter

Questions 8 - 11.

Questions 8 through 11 in Column I below are wiring diagrams of the various positions of a 4-position switch each of which is shown in simplified form by one of the circuit diagramsin Column II below. For each wiring diagram in Column I, select the simplified circuit diagram from Column II. PRINT, in the correspondingly numbered item space at the right, the letter given beside your selected circuit diagram.

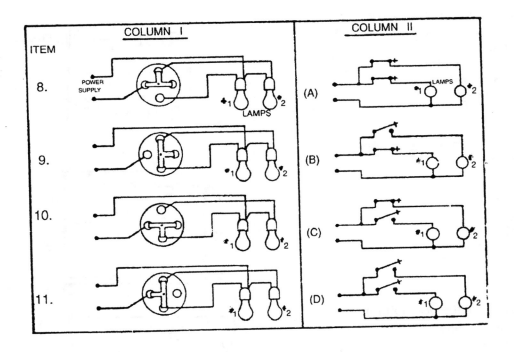

8._____

9._____

10._____

11._____

Questions 12 - 16.
Questions 12 through 16 in Column I are supply voltages each of which can be obtained by one of the dry cell battery connections in Column II. For each voltage in Column I, select the proper battery connections from Column II. *PRINT,* in the correspondingly numbered item space at the right, the letter given below your selected battery connections.

<u>COLUMN I</u>
(supply voltages)

<u>COLUMN II</u>
(battery connections)
Note: Each dry cell - 1 1/2 volts.

12. 1 1/2 volts

13. 3 volts

14. 4 1/2 volts

15. 6 volts

16. 9 volts

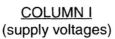
(A)

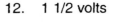
(B)

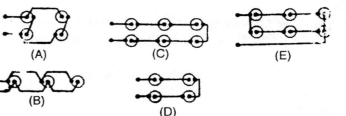
(C)   (E)

(D)

12.__

13.__

14.__

15.__

16.__

17. The sketch shows the ends of 4 bare copper wires full size with diameters as given. From left to right, the #14 wire is

● ● ● ●
$\frac{3}{16}$" $\frac{1}{8}$" $\frac{1}{16}$" $\frac{1}{32}$"

A. first
C. third

B. second
D. fourth

17.__

18. Regardless of the battery voltage, it is clear by inspection that the highest current is in the
   A. 1-ohm resistor
   B. 2-ohm resistor
   C. 3-ohm resistor
   D. 4-ohm resistor

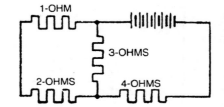
1-OHM
3-OHMS
2-OHMS   4-OHMS

18.__

19. On the transformer, the dimension marked X is
   A. 29 1/2"
   B. 27"
   C. 25 1/2"
   D. 21 1/2"

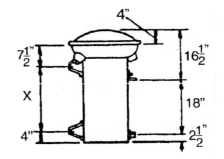
4"
$7\frac{1}{2}$" $16\frac{1}{2}$"
X   18"
4" $2\frac{1}{2}$"

19.__

20. The reading of the voltmeter in the accompanying sketch will be
   A. 0 volts
   B. 80 volts
   C. 120 volts
   D. 240 volts

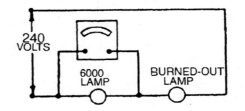
240 VOLTS
6000 LAMP   BURNED-OUT LAMP

20.__

21. The total resistance in ohms between points X and Y is
    A. 0.30
    B. 3.33
    C. 15
    D. 30

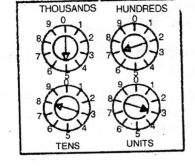

22. The resistance box shown can be set to any value of resistance up to 10,000 ohms. The reading shown is
    A. 3875
    B. 5738
    C. 5783
    D. 8375

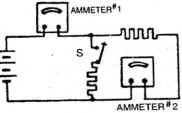

23. If switch "S" is closed, the ammeter readings will change as follows
    A. both will increase
    B. #1 only will increase
    C. both will decrease
    D. #2 only will increase

24. The reading on the meter scale shown is
    A. 56
    B. 52
    C. 51
    D. 46

25. The voltage "X" is
    A. 25
    B. 20
    C. 15
    D. 5

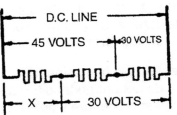

26. The two voltmeters shown are identical. If the battery voltage is 120 volts, the readings of the voltmeters should be
    A. 120 volts on each meter
    B. 60 volts on each meter
    C. 120 volts on meter #1 and 240 volts on #2
    D. 120 volts on meter #1 and zero on #2

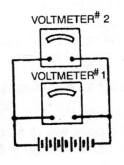

27. Standard tables are available showing the safe carrying capacity of copper wire of various sizes to avoid damage to insulation from overheating. The allowable current given is dependent on the   27.___

    A. voltage   B. length of wire
    C. type of current (a.c. or d.c.)   D. room temperature

28. A test lamp using an ordinary lamp bulb can *NOT* be used to test for   28.___

    A. live circuits   B. overloads
    C. grounds   D. blown fuses

29. Consumers are warned never to use a coin instead of a spare fuse. The reason for this warning is that   29.___

    A. the protection of the fuse will be lost
    B. additional resistance will be placed in the circuit
    C. mutilating coins is illegal
    D. shock hazard is increased

30. Maintainers are cautioned not to smoke or permit open flames in a storage battery room. The probable reason for this caution is that   30.___

    A. the liquid in the battery is inflammable
    B. the terminals are greased
    C. batteries give off an explosive gas when charging
    D. fire extinguishers are not permitted in battery rooms

31. Safety on the job is best assured by   31.___

    A. working very slowly   B. following every rule
    C. never working alone   D. keeping alert

32. If you think you have found an improvement for a piece of standard equipment used in your department, the most sensible course for you to follow would be to   32.___

    A. examine it critically before making the suggestion
    B. try to sell it to an outside company
    C. forget it because you will probably get no credit
    D. get a definite promise of reward from the management before disclosing it

33. As a helper you will be assigned to a maintainer under the general supervision of a foreman. If you do not understand the operation of some special equipment on which you work, your best procedure would be to   33.___

    A. ask the foreman since he is more competent
    B. study up at home
    C. forget the matter until you are more experienced
    D. ask the maintainer first

34. A proper use for an electrician's knife is to   34.___

    A. cut small wires
    B. mark the point where a conduit is to be cut
    C. pry out a small cartridge fuse
    D. skin wires

35. Specifying a machine screw as an 8-32 screw fixes the   35.____

    A. material
    C. diameter
    B. type of head
    D. length

36. It is good practice to connect the ground wire for a building electrical system to a   36.____

    A. gas pipe
    C. vent pipe
    B. cold water pipe
    D. steam pipe

37. When removing the insulation from a wire before making a splice, care should be taken   37.____
to avoid nicking the wire mainly because the

    A. current carrying capacity will be reduced
    B. resistance will be increased
    C. wire is more likely to break
    D. tinning on the wire will be injured

38. The term "ampere-hours" is associated with   38.____

    A. motors
    C. electromagnets
    B. transformers
    D. storage batteries

39. It is generally true that most accidents to employees result because of   39.____

    A. too heavy work schedules
    B. poor light
    C. carelessness
    D. complicated equipment

40. It is *NOT* correct to state that   40.____

    A. current flowing through a resistor causes heat
    B. rectifiers change d.c. to a.c.
    C. the conduit of an electrical system should be grounded
    D. ammeters are used in series in the circuit

41. When a d.c. voltage of 1.50 volts is applied to a certain coil, the current in the coil is 6   41.____
amperes. The resistance of this coil is

    A. 1/4 ohm   B. 4 ohms   C. 7 1/2 ohms   D. 9 ohms

Questions 42 - 50.

Questions 42 through 50 in Column I (on the next page) are electrical symbols, each of which represents one of the electrical devices shown in Column II (on the next page). For each symbol shown in Column I, select the corresponding device from Column II. *PRINT,* in the correspondingly numbered item space at the right, the letter given below your selected device.

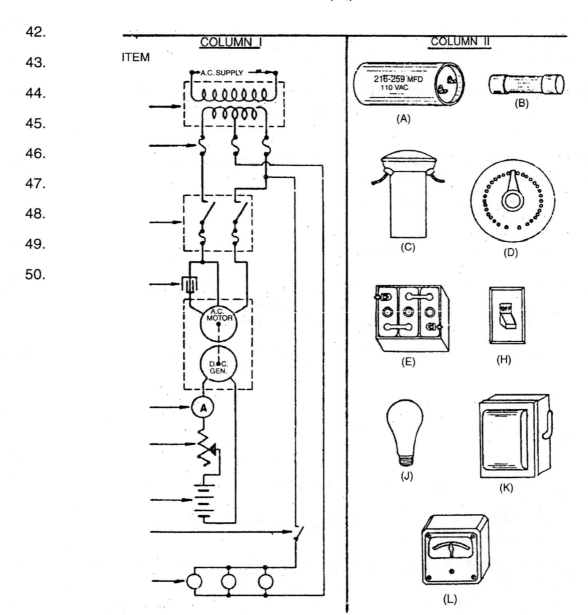

42.

43.

44.

45.

46.

47.

48.

49.

50.

42.___

43.___

44.___

45.___

46.___

47.___

48.___

49.___

50.___

KEY (CORRECT ANSWERS)

1. D	11. A	21. B	31. D	41. A
2. A	12. B	22. C	32. A	42. C
3. D	13. A	23. B	33. D	43. B
4. D	14. E	24. B	34. D	44. K
5. C	15. D	25. A	35. C	45. A
6. B	16. C	26. A	36. B	46. L
7. B	17. C	27. D	37. C	47. D
8. C	18. D	28. B	38. D	48. E
9. D	19. D	29. A	39. C	49. H
10. B	20. A	30. C	40. B	50. J

EXAMINATION SECTION
TEST 1

DIRECTIONS: Each question or incomplete statement is followed by several suggested answers or completions. Select the one that *BEST* answers the question or completes the statement. *PRINT THE LETTER OF THE CORRECT ANSWER IN THE SPACE AT THE RIGHT.*

1. The core of an electro-magnet is usually

    A. aluminum   B. lead   C. brass   D. iron

1._____

2. The purpose of applying artificial respiration to the victim of an electric shock is to

    A. restore blood circulation
    B. avoid excessive loss of blood
    C. keep the victim warm
    D. supply oxygen to the lungs

2._____

3. Electrical maintenance workers whose duties require them to be on the tracks in the subway generally work In pairs. Of the following possible reasons for having the two men work together, the *LEAST* likely is that

    A. the tools and equipment are too much for one man to carry
    B. it provides better protection against vandalism
    C. some of the tests and maintenance work require two men
    D. the men can help each other in case of accident

3._____

4. A stranded wire is given the same size designation as a solid wire if it has the same

    A. cross-sectional area   B. weight per foot
    C. overall diameter   D. strength

4._____

5. Safety regulations prohibit testing even a 20-volt light socket with the fingers to see whether the socket is alive. The main reason for this prohibition is that

    A. such action can become a bad working habit
    B. a 20-volt shock is often fatal
    C. sockets usually have sharp edges
    D. the skin will become less sensitive to higher voltages

5._____

6. One advantage of cutting 1" rigid conduit with a hacksaw rather than with a 3-wheel pipe cutter is that

    A. the cut can be made with less exertion
    B. the pipe is not squeezed out of round
    C. less reaming is required after the cut
    D. no vise is needed

6._____

7. Rigid conduit used in the subway is galvanized inside and outside. The purpose of the galvanizing is to

    A. protect the wiring by covering rough spots
    B. improve the appearance where the conduit is exposed to view
    C. protect the conduit against corrosion
    D. provide good contact for grounding the conduit

7._____

8. If a hacksaw blade becomes worn so that the teeth are no longer properly set, the   8.__

    A. blade will tend to bind in the cut
    B. cut will have jagged edges
    C. cutting must all be done on the back stroke
    D. blade will lose its temper

9. If you and another helper are assigned to a hard and tedious job and your co-worker is   9.__
not doing a reasonable share of the work, your best procedure is to

    A. slow down to his rate
    B. do your share and quit
    C. try to persuade him to do his share
    D. stop and register a complaint with the foreman before continuing

10. The most informative way for John Doe, the helper on duty at the 19th Street Lighting   10.__
Section headquarters in the subway, to answer the telephone would be to say,

    A. "19th Street, who's calling?"
    B. "John Doe speaking."
    C. "Lighting Section, 19th Street."
    D. "Hello, this is Lighting Section."

11. Assume that the field leads of a large, completely disconnected d.c. motor are not tagged   11.__
or otherwise marked. You could readily tell the shunt field leads from the series field
leads by the

    A. length of the leads
    B. size of wire
    C. thickness of insulation
    D. type of insulation

12. Standard electrician's pliers should *NOT* be used to   12.__

    A. bend thin sheet metal
    B. crush Insulation on wires to be skinned
    C. cut off nail points sticking through a board
    D. hold a wire in position for soldering

13. The device used to change a.c. to d.c. is a   13.__

    A. frequency   B. regulator
    C. transformer   D. rectifier

14. The chief advantage of using stranded rather than solid conductors for electrical wiring is   14.__
that stranded conductors are

    A. more flexible   B. easier to skin
    C. smaller   D. stronger

15. One identifying feature of a squirrel-cage induction motor is that it has no

    A. windings on the stationary part
    B. commutator or slip rings
    C. air gap
    D. iron core in the rotating part

15._____

16. It is advisable to close a knife switch firmly and rapidly because then there is less

    A. danger of shock to the operator
    B. chance of making an error
    C. mechanical wear of the contacts
    D. likelihood of arcing

16._____

17. If a cartridge fuse is hot to the touch when you remove it to do some maintenance on the circuit, this most probably indicates that the

    A. voltage of the circuit is too high
    B. fuse clips do not make good contact
    C. equipment on the circuit starts and stops frequently
    D. fuse is oversize for the circuit

17._____

18. The instrument most commonly used to determine the state of charge of a lead-acid storage battery is the

    A. thermometer   B. hydrometer
    C. voltmeter   D. ammeter

18._____

19. Smoking is forbidden in rooms housing storage batteries mainly because of the inflammable gas given off when the batteries are being charged. This gas is

    A. hydrogen   B. carbon monoxide
    C. ammonia   D. chlorine

19._____

20. Rigid conduit must be so installed as to prevent the collection of water in it between outlets. In order to meet this requirement, the conduit should NOT have a

    A. low point between successive outlets
    B. high point between successive outlets
    C. low point at an outlet
    D. high point at an outlet

20._____

21. When a test lamp is connected to the two ends of a cartridge fuse on an operating switchboard, the indication in ALL cases will be that this fuse is

    A. blown if the test lamp remains dark
    B. good if the test lamp lights
    C. blown if the test lamp lights
    D. good if the test lamp remains dark

21._____

22. If one copper wire has a diameter of 0.128 inch, and another copper wire has a diameter of 0.064 inch, the resistance of 1,000 feet of the first wire compared to the same length of the second wire is

    A. one half   B. one quarter
    C. double   D. four times

22._____

23. The area of a circle having a diameter of one inch is closest to ___23.___

    A. 3/4 square inch
    B. 1 square inch
    C. 1 1/3 square inches
    D. 1 1/2 square inches

24. If the allowable current In a copper bus bar is 1,000 amperes per square inch of cross-section, the width of a standard 1/4" bus bar designed to carry 1500 amperes would be ___24.___

    A. 2"
    B. 4"
    C. 6"
    D. 8"

25. It is now possible to obtain a 200-watt light-bulb that is as small in all dimensions as the standard 150-watt light-bulb. The principal advantage to users resulting from this reduction in size is that ___25.___

    A. maintenance electricians can carry many more light-bulbs
    B. two sizes of light-bulbs can be kept in the same storage space
    C. the higher wattage bulb can now fit into certain lighting fixtures
    D. less breakage is apt to occur in handling

26. A carbon brush in a d.c. motor should exert a pressure of about 1 1/2 lbs. per square inch on the commutator.
    A much lighter pressure would be most likely to result in ___26.___

    A. sparking at the commutator
    B. vibration of the armature
    C. the brush getting out of line
    D. excessive wear of the brush holder

27. The number of watts of heat given off by a resistor is expressed by the formula I^2R. If 10 volts is applied to a 5-ohm resistor, the heat given off will be ___27.___

    A. 500 watts
    B. 250 watts
    C. 50 watts
    D. 20 watts

Questions 28 - 36.

Questions 28 through 36 in Column I are electrical instruments and devices each of which is represented by one of the symbols in the schematic wiring diagram shown in Column II. For each instrument or device in Column I, select the corresponding symbol from Column II. *PRINT*, in the correspondingly numbered item space at the right, the letter given beside your selected symbol.

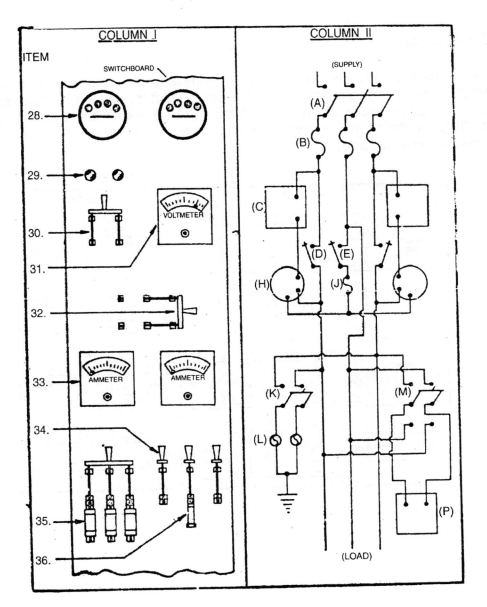

28.____

29.____

30.____

31.____

32.____

33.____

34.____

35.____

36.____

Questions 37 -40.

Questions 37 through 40 in Column I are wiring diagrams of the various positions of two rotary snap-switches each of which is shown in simplified form by one of the circuit diagrams in Column II. For each wiring diagram in Column I, select the simplified circuit diagram from Column II. *PRINT,* in the correspondingly number item space at the right, the letter given beside your selected circuit diagram.

37.____

38.____

39.____

40.____

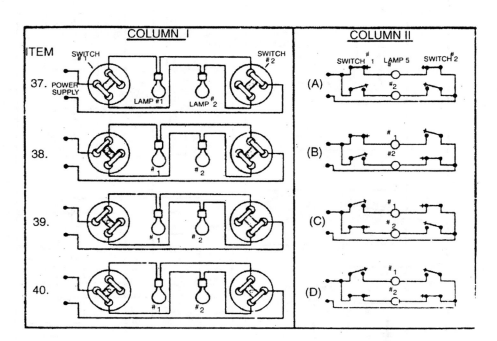

Questions 41 - 45.

Questions 41 through 45 in Column I are rating-terms each of which is commonly used in association with one of the electrical devices listed in Column II. For each rating-term in Column I, select the most closely associated electrical device from Column II. *PRINT,* in the correspondingly number item space at the right, the letter given beside your selected device.

Column I (rating-terms)	Column II (electrical devices)	
41. 120 watts; 5 ohms	A. resistor	41._____
42. 120 to 13,800 volts	B. toggle switch	42._____
43. 120 volts; 100 watts	C. transformer	43._____
44. 120 volts; 100 amp.-hrs.	D. light-bulb	44._____
45. 120 volts; 10 amp.	E. storage battery	45._____

46. Assuming that the same kind of insulating material is used on each of the four copper conductors shown, the one intended for the highest voltage service is number
   A. 1
   B. 2
   C. 3
   D. 4

46._____

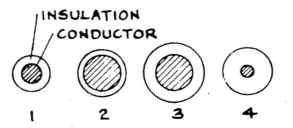

47. The convenience outlet that is known as a *POLARIZED* outlet is number
   A. 1
   B. 2
   C. 3
   D. 4

47._____

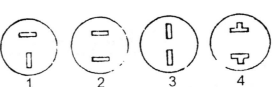
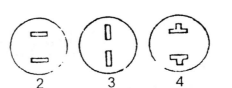

48. The group of 1 1/2-volt dry cells which is properly connected to deliver 6 volts is number
   A. 1
   B. 2
   C. 3
   D. 4

48._____

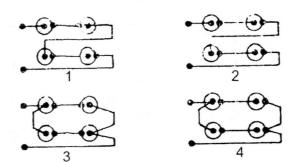

49. Each of the four sketches shows the proper schematic connections for one kind of d.c. motor. The one showing the connections for a shunt motor is number
    A. 1
    B. 2
    C. 3
    D. 4

49.____

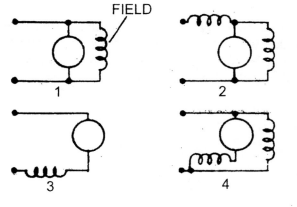

50. The four illustrations show pairs of equal strength permanent magnets on pivots, each magnet being held in the position shown by a mechanical locking device. When they are mechanically unlocked, the magnets which are *LEAST* likely to change their positions are pair number
    A. 1
    B. 2
    C. 3
    D. 4

50.____

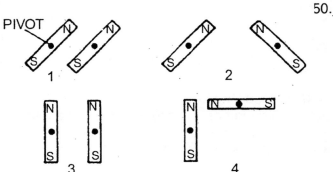

KEY (CORRECT ANSWERS)

1.	D	11.	B	21.	C	31.	P	41.	A
2.	D	12.	C	22.	B	32.	M	42.	C
3.	B	13.	D	23.	A	33.	C	43.	D
4.	A	14.	A	24.	C	34.	D	44.	E
5.	A	15.	B	25.	C	35.	B	45.	B
6.	C	16.	D	26.	A	36.	J	46.	D
7.	C	17.	B	27.	D	37.	C	47.	A
8.	A	18.	B	28.	H	38.	A	48.	B
9.	C	19.	A	29.	L	39.	B	49.	A
10.	C	20.	A	30.	K	40.	D	50.	C

TEST 2

DIRECTIONS: Each question or incomplete statement is followed by several suggested answers or completions. Select the one that *BEST* answers the question or completes the statement. *PRINT THE LETTER OF THE CORRECT ANSWER IN THE SPACE AT THE RIGHT.*

1. If the currents in resistors nos. 1, 2, and 3 are 4.8, 7.5, and 6.2 amperes respectively, then the current (in amperes) in resistor no. 4 is
   A. 1.3
   B. 2.7
   C. 3.5
   D. 6.1

1.____

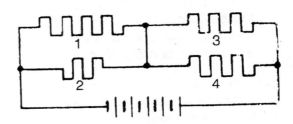

2. If the mercury switch is turned to the horizontal position, the mercury will flow and break the connection between the lead-in wires, thus opening the circuit. By logical reasoning, such a switch would be most useful when

2.____

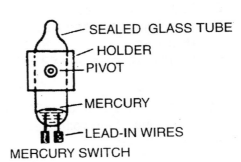

SEALED GLASS TUBE
HOLDER
PIVOT
MERCURY
LEAD-IN WIRES
MERCURY SWITCH

   A. the circuit must be opened quickly
   B. there is likely to be explosive gas near the switch location
   C. there is no restriction on noise
   D. the switch need not be operated often

3. The device shown is clearly intended for use in electrical construction to
   A. support conduit on a wall
   B. join cable to a terminal block
   C. ground a wire to a water pipe
   D. attach a chain-hung lighting fixture to an outlet box

3.____

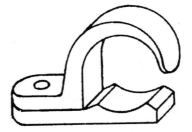

4. The fitting shown is used in electrical construction to
   A. clamp two adjacent junction boxes together
   B. act as a ground clamp for the conduit system
   C. attach flexible metallic conduit to a junction box
   D. protect exposed wires where they pass through a wall

4.____

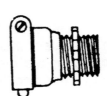

5. The electrical connector shown would most likely be used in a power plant to connect
   A. two branch cables to a main cable
   B. a single cable to the terminals of two devices
   C. a single cable to a flat bus bar
   D. a round bus bar to a flat one

5.____

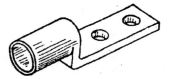

6. If switch S is closed, the resulting change in the ammeter readings will be that
   A. both will increase
   B. both will decrease
   C. #1 will increase and #2 will decrease
   D. #1 will decrease and #2 will increase

6.____

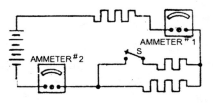

7. If the 10-ohm resistor marked X burns out, the reading of the voltmeter will become
   A. 0
   B. 20
   C. 80
   D. 100

7.____

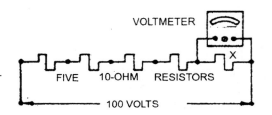

8. The width of the bar, in inches, is
   A. 1 1/8
   B. 1 5/16
   C. 1 7/16
   D. 2 5/16

8.____

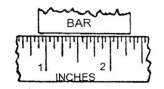

9. The total resistance, in ohms, between points X and Y is
   A. 2.5
   B. 5
   C. 10
   D. 20

9.____

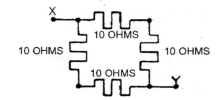

10. The range of both voltmeters shown is 0-150 volts. In this case, the a.c. meter will indicate the correct voltage and the d.c. meter will indicate
    A. the same
    B. a few volts more
    C. a few volts less
    D. zero

10.____

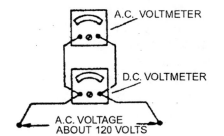

11. The six wires shown are to be properly connected so that the lighting fixture can be controlled by a single-pole on-off switch. The correct connections in accordance with established good practice are

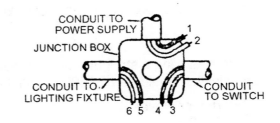

CONDUIT TO POWER SUPPLY
JUNCTION BOX
CONDUIT TO LIGHTING FIXTURE
CONDUIT TO SWITCH
1 2 6 5 4 3

11.____

    A.   1 to 3 and 5; 2 to 4 and 6
    B.   1 to 5; 2 to 3; 4 to 6
    C.   1 to 3 and 6; 2 to 4 and 5
    D.   1 to 3; 4 to 5; 2 to 6

12. In the right-angled triangle shown, the angle marked X is

12.____

    A.   45°
    B.   60°
    C.   75°
    D.   90°

(Triangle shown with 30° angle and angle X)

13. The distance from the top of the desk to the bottom of the lighting fixture is

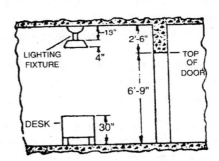

LIGHTING FIXTURE — 13" — 4"; TOP OF DOOR; 2'-6"; 6'-9"; DESK — 30"

13.____

    A.   94"
    B.   81"
    C.   72"
    D.   64"

14. When the movable arm of the uniformly wound resistor is in the position shown, the resistance in ohms between terminals 2 and 3 is

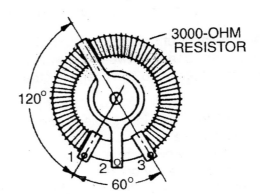

3000-OHM RESISTOR
120°
60°
1 2 3

14.____

    A.   2000
    B.   1800
    C.   1500
    D.   1200

15. If each of the 19 strands of the conductor shown has a diameter of 0.024", and the thickness of the insulation is 0.047", the diameter over the insulation is

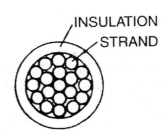

INSULATION
STRAND

15.____

    A.   0.107"
    B.   0.167"
    C.   0.214"
    D.   0.238"

16. After no. 4, the next larger American Wire Gage size is no. 16.___

    A. 2   B. 3   C. 5   D. 6

17. When steadying a straight wooden ladder for a co-worker who is on it chipping a con- 17.___
crete wall, it would be *LEAST* essential for you to wear

    A. rubber gloves   B. hard top shoes
    C. goggles   D. a helmet

18. It would *NOT* be good practice to use the cutting blade of an electrician's knife to 18.___

    A. cut a template out of cardboard
    B. sharpen a pencil
    C. cut copper wires
    D. remove the braid from an insulated wire

19. You are more likely to receive a shock as the result of a wiring defect in a portable electri- 19.___
cal device than as the result of a similar defect in a permanently installed device. This is
so primarily because the

    A. workers on permanent installations are more careful
    B. insulation on portable equipment is usually thinner
    C. metal parts of portable equipment are usually light weight
    D. metal frames of permanent installations are usually grounded

20. If a co-worker is in contact with the 600-volt third rail in the subway, your first action 20.___
should be to either try to free the man from contact or cut off the power. The action to be
taken in a particular case will depend primarily on whether

    A. cutting off the power will interfere with train operation
    B. the means of cutting off the power Is nearby
    C. there is any arcing at the point of contact
    D. you can free the man in time to do any good

21. When a number of rubber insulated wires are being pulled into a run of conduit having 21.___
several sharp bends between the two pull boxes, the pulling is likely to be hard and the
wires are subjected to considerable strain. For these reasons it is advisable in such a
case to

    A. push the wires into the feed end of the conduit at the same time that pulling is
being done
    B. pull in only one wire at a time
    C. use extra heavy grease
    D. pull the wires back a few inches after each forward pull to gain momentum

22. The plug of a portable tool should be removed from the convenience outlet by grasping 22.___
the plug and not by pulling on the cord because

    A. the plug is easier to grip than the cord
    B. pulling on the cord may allow the plug to fall on the floor and break
    C. pulling on the cord may break the wires off the
    D. plug terminals
    E. the plug is generally better insulated than the cord

23. The best *IMMEDIATE* first aid if electrolyte splashes into the eyes when filling a storage battery is to

    A. bandage the eyes to keep out light
    B. wipe the eyes dry with a soft towel
    C. induce tears to flow by staring at a bright light
    D. bathe the eyes with plenty of clean water

23._____

24. Extreme care must be taken when cleaning electrical machine parts indoors with carbon tetrachloride mainly because the fumes

    A. are poisonous
    B. are highly flammable
    C. attack insulation
    D. conduct electricity

24._____

25. When using a pipe wrench, the hand should be placed so as to pull instead of push on the wrench. The basis for this recommendation is that there is less likelihood of

    A. the wrench slipping
    B. injury to the hand if the wrench slips
    C. injury to the pipe if the wrench slips
    D. stripped pipe threads

25._____

26. In telephoning for assistance because of an accident to a fellow-employee, it is probably most important for you to report the

    A. name of the injured man
    B. time when the accident occurred
    C. cause of the accident
    D. location of the injured man

26._____

27. The electrical power for each section of the subway signal system is arranged to come from either one of two supply feeders. The most likely reason for this arrangement is to

    A. divide the load between two power plants
    B. provide continuing service if one feeder goes dead
    C. keep the supply voltage as low as possible
    D. avoid the use of very large cables

27._____

28. Present practice with respect to subway lighting switchboards is to make them "dead front." This means that the front of the switchboard has no

    A. metal parts fastened to it
    B. exposed live parts on it
    C. operating handles extending through it
    D. circuit identification markings on it

28._____

29. High-voltage switches in power plants are commonly so constructed that their contacts are submerged in oil. The purpose of the oil is to

    A. help quench arcing
    B. lubricate the contacts
    C. cool the switch mechanism
    D. insulate the contacts from the switch framework

29._____

30. One type of fire extinguisher used in the subway consists of a steel tank containing com-   30.__
    pressed carbon dioxide; it has a valve at the top to which is connected a hose and a
    directing nozzle. The logical way to tell whether such an extinguisher is fully charged is to

    A. tap it lightly   B. check the inspection tag
    C. weigh it   D. try it out on a small fire

31. In a storage battery installation consisting of twenty 2-volt cells connected in series, a   31.__
    leak develops in one of the cells and all the electrolyte runs out of it. The terminal voltage
    across the twenty cells will now be

    A. 40   B. 38   C. 2   D. 0

32. If your foreman gives you an oral order which you do not understand, you should   32.__

    A. ask the foreman to put the order in writing
    B. ask the foreman to explain further
    C. ask a fellow employee what he thinks the foreman meant
    D. use your best judgment as that is all that can be expected

33. It is advisable to use a wooden rather than a steel rule when making measurements in   33.__
    the vicinity of electrical machinery. One good reason for this advice is that a wooden rule

    A. will not conduct electricity
    B. can be held in a position by using only one hand
    C. cannot become magnetized
    D. will not damage the machinery if it becomes caught

Items 34 -39.

Items 34 through 39 in Column I are insulating materials each of which is commonly employed
for one of the uses listed in Column II. For each insulating material in Column I select its most
common use from Column II. *PRINT,* in the correspondingly number item space at the right, the
letter given beside your selected use.

Column I   Column II
(insulating materials)   (uses)

34. Porcelain   A. knive-switch handles   34.__

35. Transite   B. commutator-bar separators   35.__

36. Wood   C. high voltage line insulators   36.__

37. Soft rubber   D. wire and cable insulation   37.__

38. Fiber   E. cartridge fuse cases   38.__

39. Mica   F. arc chutes   39.__

40. If the blade in a hacksaw snaps in two when making a cut, the cause is *NOT* likely to be that the

    A. teeth were too coarse for work
    B. pressure applied was too great
    C. saw was twisted in the cut
    D. blade was too short for the job

40.____

41. When removing the insulation from a wire before making a splice, care should be taken to avoid nicking the wire mainly because then the

    A. current carrying capacity will be reduced
    B. resistance will be increased
    C. insulation will be harder to remove
    D. wire is more likely to break

41.____

42. Good practice dictates that an adjustable open end wrench should be used primarily when the

    A. nut to be turned is soft and must not be scored
    B. proper size of fixed wrench is not available
    C. extra leverage is needed
    D. location is cramped permitting only a small turning angle

42.____

43. Insulated electrical cables in the subway are sometimes suspended from a tightly strung messenger wire which is supported on brackets attached to the subway structure at intervals of 10 to 20 feet; the electrical cables are strapped to the messenger wire every few inches. By logical reasoning, it is clear that such electrical cables are not suspended overhead without being supported by a messenger wire because the

    A. messenger wire is needed as a continuous ground return
    B. current carrying capacity of unsupported electrical cables would be lower
    C. messenger wire places less strain on the structure
    D. longer spans of electrical cables would sag too much

43.____

44. It would generally be poor practice to use ordinary slip-joint pliers to

    A. pull a small nail
    B. bend a wire
    C. remove a cotter pin
    D. tighten a machine bolt

44.____

45. The a.c. motor which has exactly the same speed at full-load as at no load is the

    A. synchronous motor
    B. repulsion motor
    C. induction motor
    D. condenser motor

45.____

46. A metal bushing is usually screwed on to the end of rigid conduit inside of a junction box. The bushing serves to

    A. center the wires in the conduit
    B. separate the wires where they leave the conduit
    C. protect the wires against abrasion
    D. prevent sagging of the conduit

46.____

47. The proper abrasive for cleaning the commutator of a d.c. generator is

    A. steel wool
    B. emery cloth
    C. sand paper
    D. soapstone

47.____

121

48. If a "live" 120-volt d.c. lighting circuit is connected to the 120-volt winding of an otherwise disconnected power transformer, the result will be

    A. blowing of the d.c. circuit fuse
    B. magnetization of the transformer case
    C. sparking at the transformer secondary terminals
    D. burning out of lights on the d.c. circuit

48.___

49. Threaded joints in rigid conduit runs are made watertight through the use of

    A. petroleum jelly   B. solder
    C. red lead   D. paraffin wax

49.___

50. The most important reason for insisting on neatness in maintenance quarters is that it

    A. decreases the chances of accidents to employees
    B. makes for good employee morale
    C. prevents tools from becoming rusty
    D. increases the available storage space

50.___

KEY (CORRECT ANSWERS)

1. D	11. D	21. A	31. D	41. D
2. B	12. B	22. C	32. B	42. B
3. A	13. D	23. D	33. A	43. D
4. C	14. B	24. A	34. C	44. D
5. C	15. C	25. B	35. F	45. A
6. A	16. B	26. D	36. A	46. C
7. D	17. A	27. B	37. D	47. C
8. C	18. C	28. B	38. E	48. A
9. C	19. D	29. A	39. B	49. C
10. D	20. B	30. C	40. D	50. A

EXAMINATION SECTION
TEST 1

DIRECTIONS: Each question or incomplete statement is followed by several suggested answers or completions. Select the one that BEST answers the question or completes the statement. *PRINT THE LETTER OF THE CORRECT ANSWER IN THE SPACE AT THE RIGHT.*

Questions 1-8.

DIRECTIONS: Questions 1 through 8 involve tests on the fuse box arrangement shown below. All tests are to be performed with a neon tester or a lamp test bank consisting of two 6-watt, 120-volt lamps connected in series. Do not make any assumptions about the conditions of the circuits. Draw your conclusions only from the information obtained with the neon tester or the two-lamp test bank, applied to the circuits as called for.

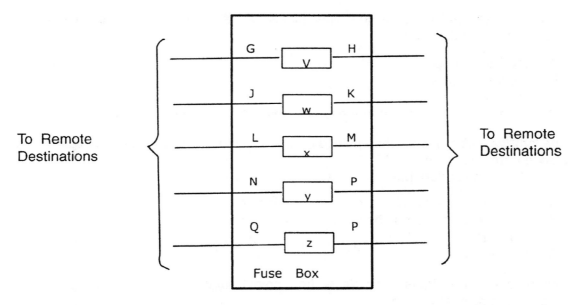

1. The two lamp test bank is placed from point G to joint J, and both lamps light.   1._____
    One of the lamps is momentarily removed from its socket; during that instant, the other lamp in the series-connected test bank should

    A. go dark
    B. get dimmer
    C. remain at same brightness
    D. get brighter

2. The test bank with two 60-watt, 120-volt lamps in series should be used on circuits with   2._____

    A. wattages only from 60 to 120 watts
    B. wattages only from 0 to 120 watts
    C. voltages only from 120 to 240 volts
    D. voltages only from 0 to 240 volts

3. The neon tester is placed from point G to point J and only one-half of the neon tester lights.
It should be concluded that

    A. half of the tester has gone bad
    B. a wire has become disconnected in the circuit
    C. the voltage is AC
    D. the voltage is DC

3.__

4. If both lamps in the test bank light when placed directly across one of the above fuses, it should be concluded that

    A. the fuse is good
    B. the fuse is blown
    C. the fuse is overrated
    D. further tests have to be made to determine the condition of the fuse

4.__

5. If the lamp test bank does not light when placed directly across one of the above fuses, it should be concluded that

    A. the fuse is good
    B. the fuse is blown
    C. the fuse is overrated
    D. further tests have to be made to determine the condition of the fuse

5.__

6. The lamp test bank lights when placed from point G to point J but does not light when placed from point H to point J.
It should be concluded that

    A. the wire to point H has become disconnected
    B. the wire to point J has become disconnected
    C. fuse v is bad
    D. fuse w is bad

6.__

7. The lamp test bank lights when placed from point L to point N but does not light when placed from point M to point P.
It should be concluded that

    A. both fuses x and y are bad
    B. either fuse x or fuse y is bad or both are bad
    C. both fuses x and y are good
    D. these tests do not indicate the condition of any fuse

7.__

8. The lamp test bank is placed from point L to point N, then from N to point Q, and finally from point L to point Q. In each case, both lamps light to full brightness.
It should be concluded that points L, N, and Q have

    A. three-phase, 120 volts, AC, line-to-line
    B. plus and minus 120 volts, DC
    C. three-phase, 208 volts, AC
    D. plus and minus 240 volts, DC

8.__

9. The resistance of a copper wire to the flow of electricity _____ as the _____ of the wire _____.   9.____

    A. increases; diameter; increases
    B. decreases; diameter; decreases
    C. decreases; length; increases
    D. increases; length; increases

10. Where galvanized steel conduit is used, the PRIMARY purpose of the galvanizing is to   10.____

    A. increase mechanical strength
    B. retard rusting
    C. provide a good surface for painting
    D. provide good electrical contact for grounding

11. The lamps used for station and tunnel lighting in subways are generally operated at slightly less than their rated voltage.   11.____
The LOGICAL reason for this is to

    A. prevent overloading of circuits
    B. increase the life of the lamps
    C. decrease glare
    D. obtain a more even distribution of light

12. The CORRECT method of measuring the power taken by an AC electric motor is to use a   12.____

    A. wattmeter   B. voltmeter and an ammeter
    C. power factor meter   D. tachometer

13. Wood ladders should NOT be painted because the paint may   13.____

    A. deteriorate the wood   B. make ladders slippery
    C. be inflammable   D. cover cracks or defects

14. Goggles would be LEAST necessary when   14.____

    A. recharging soda-acid fire extinguishers
    B. chipping stone
    C. putting electrolyte into an Edison battery
    D. scraping rubber insulation from a wire

15. The number and type of precautions to be taken on a job generally depend LEAST on the   15.____

    A. nature of the job
    B. length of time the job is expected to last
    C. kind of tools and materials being used
    D. location of the work

16. When training workers in the use of tools and equipment, safety precautions related to their use should be FIRST mentioned   16.____

    A. in the introductory training session before the workers begin to use the equipment or tools
    B. during training sessions when workers practice operating the tools or equipment

C.   after the workers are qualified to use the equipment in their daily tasks
D.   when an agency safety bulletin related to the tools and equipment is received

17.   Artificial respiration should be started immediately on a man who has suffered an electric   17.___
shock if he is

A.   *unconscious* and breathing
B.   *unconscious* and not breathing
C.   *conscious* and in a daze
D.   *conscious* and badly burned

18.   The fuse of a certain circuit has blown and is replaced with a fuse of the same rating   18.___
which also blows when the switch is closed.
In this case,

A.   a fuse of higher current rating should be used
B.   a fuse of higher voltage rating should be used
C.   the fuse should be temporarily replaced by a heavy piece of wire
D.   the circuit should be checked

19.   Operating an incandescent electric light bulb at less than its rated voltage will result in   19.___

A.   shorter life and brighter light
B.   longer life and dimmer light
C.   brighter light and longer life
D.   dimmer light and shorter life

20.   In order to control a lamp from two different positions, it is necessary to use   20.___

A.   two single pole switches
B.   one single pole switch and one four-way switch
C.   two three-way switches
D.   one single pole switch and one four-way switch

21.   One method of testing fuses is to con-   21.___
nect a pair of test lamps in the circuit in
such a manner that the test lamp will light
up if the fuse is good and will remain dark
if the fuse is bad. In the illustration at the
right, 1 and 2 are fuses.
In order to test if fuse 1 is bad, test
lamps should be connected between

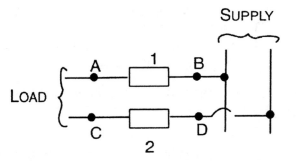

A.   A and B
B.   B and D
C.   A and D
D.   C and B

22.   The PRINCIPAL reason for the grounding of electrical equipment and circuits is to   22.___

A.   prevent short circuits   B.   insure safety from shock
C.   save power   D.   increase voltage

23. An interlock is generally installed on electronic equipment to   23.____

    A. prevent loss of power
    B. maintain VHF frequencies
    C. keep the vacuum tubes lit
    D. prevent electric shock during maintenance operations

24. A flame should not be used to inspect the electrolyte level in a lead-acid battery because   24.____
the battery cells give off highly flammable

    A. hydrogen   B. lead oxide
    C. lithium   D. xenon

25. The purpose of the third prong in a three-prong male electric plug used in a 120 volt circuit is to   25.____

    A. make a firm connection   B. strengthen the plug
    C. ground to prevent shock   D. act as a transducer

KEY (CORRECT ANSWERS)

1.	A		11.	B
2.	D		12.	A
3.	D		13.	D
4.	B		14.	D
5.	D		15.	B
6.	C		16.	A
7.	B		17.	B
8.	C		18.	D
9.	D		19.	B
10.	B		20.	C

21.	C
22.	B
23.	D
24.	A
25.	C

TEST 2

DIRECTIONS: Each question or incomplete statement is followed by several suggested answers or completions. Select the one that BEST answers the question or completes the statement. *PRINT THE LETTER OF THE CORRECT ANSWER IN THE SPACE AT THE RIGHT.*

1. The BEST procedure to follow when replacing a blown fuse is to   1.___

    A. immediately replace it with the same size fuse
    B. immediately replace it with a larger size fuse
    C. immediately replace it with a smaller size fuse
    D. correct the cause of the fuse failure and replace it with the correct size

2. The amperage rating of the fuse to be used in an electrical circuit is determined by the   2.___

    A. size of the connected load
    B. size of the wire in the circuit
    C. voltage of the circuit
    D. ambient temperature

3. In a 208 volt, three-phase, 4 wire circuit, the voltage, in volts, from any line to the   3.___
   grounded neutral is APPROXIMATELY

    A. 208   B. 150   C. 120   D. zero

4. The device commonly used to change an AC voltage to a DC voltage is called a   4.___

    A. transformer   B. rectifier
    C. relay   D. capacitor or condenser

5. Where conduit enters a knock-out in an outlet box, it should be provided with a   5.___

    A. bushing on the inside and locknut on the outside
    B. locknut on the inside and bushing on the outside
    C. union on the outside and a nipple on the inside
    D. nipple on the outside and a union on the inside

6. The electric circuit to a ten kilowatt electric hot water heater which is automatically con-   6.___
   trolled by an aquastat will also require a

    A. transistor   B. choke coil
    C. magnetic contactor   D. limit switch

7. An electric power consumption meter USUALLY indicates the power used in   7.___

    A. watts   B. volt-hours
    C. amperes   D. kilowatt-hours

8. Of the following sizes of copper wire, the one which can SAFELY carry the greatest   8.___
   amount of amperes is

    A. 14 ga. stranded   B. 12 ga. stranded
    C. 12 ga. solid   D. 10 ga. solid

9. If a 110 volt lamp were used on a 220 volt circuit, the 9.____

    A. fuse would burn out   B. lamp would burn out
    C. line would overheat   D. lamp would flicker

10. The material which is LEAST likely to be found in use as the outer covering of rubber   10.____
insulated wires or cables is

    A. cotton   B. varnished cambric
    C. lead   D. neoprene

11. In measuring to determine the size of a stranded insulated conductor, the PROPER   11.____
place to use the wire gauge is on

    A. the insulation
    B. the outer covering
    C. the stranded conductor
    D. one strand of the conductor

12. Rubber insulation on an electrical conductor would MOST quickly be damaged by contin-   12.____
uous contact with

    A. acid   B. water   C. oil   D. alkali

13. If a fuse clip becomes hot under normal circuit load, the MOST probable cause is that the   13.____

    A. clip makes poor contact with the fuse ferrule
    B. circuit wires are too small
    C. current rating of the fuse is too high
    D. voltage rating of the fuse is too low

14. If the input to a 10 to 1 step-down transformer is 15 amperes at 2400 volts, the second-   14.____
ary output would be NEAREST to _____ amperes at _____ volts.

    A. 1.5; 24,000   B. 150; 240
    C. 1.5; 240   D. 150; 24,000

15. In a two-wire electrical system, the color of the wire which is grounded is USUALLY   15.____

    A. white   B. red   C. black   D. green

16. It is generally recommended that wooden ladders be kept coated with a suitable protec-   16.____
tive coating.
The one of the following which is NOT a suitable protective coating is

    A. clear lacquer   B. clear varnish
    C. linseed oil   D. paint

17. The tool you should use to mend metal by soldering is   17.____

A.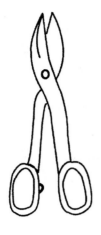

B.

C.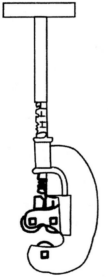

D.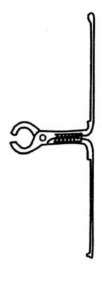

18. The one of the following that is NOT part of an electric motor is a   18.__

    A. brush   B. rheostat   C. pole   D. commutator

19. An electrical transformer would be used to   19.__

    A. change current from AC to DC
    B. raise or lower the power
    C. raise or lower the voltage
    D. change the frequency

20. The piece of equipment that would be rated in ampere hours is a   20.__

    A. storage battery   B. bus bar
    C. rectifier   D. capacitor

21. A ballast is a necessity in a(n)   21.__

    A. motor generator set
    B. fluorescent lighting system
    C. oil circuit breaker
    D. synchronous converter

22. The power factor in an AC circuit is on when

    A. no current is flowing
    B. the voltage at the source is a minimum
    C. the voltage and current are in phase
    D. there is no load

22._____

23. Neglecting the internal resistance in the battery, the current flowing through the battery shown at the right is _____ amp.
    A. 3
    B. 6
    C. 9
    D. 12

23._____

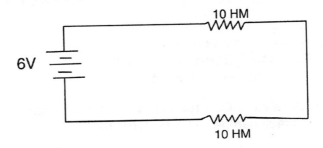

24. Using a fuse with a LARGER rated capacity than that of the circuit is

    A. *advisable;* such use prevents the fuse from blowing
    B. *advisable;* larger capacity fuses last longer than smaller capacity fuses
    C. *inadvisable;* larger capacity fuses are more expensive than smaller capacity fuses
    D. *inadvisable;* such use may cause a fire

24._____

25. You can MOST easily tell when a screw-in type fuse has blown because the center of the strip of metal in the fuse is

    A. broken
    C. nicked
    B. visible
    D. cool to the touch

25._____

KEY (CORRECT ANSWERS)

1.	D		11.	D
2.	B		12.	C
3.	C		13.	A
4.	B		14.	B
5.	A		15.	A
6.	C		16.	D
7.	D		17.	B
8.	D		18.	B
9.	B		19.	C
10.	B		20.	A

21.	B
22.	C
23.	A
24.	D
25.	A

TEST 3

DIRECTIONS: Each question or incomplete statement is followed by several suggested answers or completions. Select the one that BEST answers the question or completes the statement. *PRINT THE LETTER OF THE CORRECT ANSWER IN THE SPACE AT THE RIGHT.*

1. The ordinary single-pole flush wall type switch must be connected   1.__

    A. across the line
    B. in the hot conductor
    C. in the grounded conductor
    D. in the white conductor

2. A DC shunt motor runs in the wrong direction.   2.__
   This fault can be CORRECTED by

    A. reversing the connections of both the field and the armature
    B. interchanging the connections of either main or auxiliary windings
    C. interchanging the connections to either the field or the armature windings
    D. interchanging the connections to the line of the power leads

3. The MOST common type of motor that can be used with both AC and DC sources is the   3.__
   _____ motor.

    A. compound   B. repulsion   C. series   D. shunt

4. A fluorescent fixture in a new building has been in use for several months without trouble.   4.__
   Recently, the ends of the fluorescent lamp have remained lighted when the light was
   switched off.
   The BEST way to clear up this trouble is to replace the

    A. lamp   B. ballast   C. starter   D. sockets

5. A ballast is a part of a(n)   5.__

    A. fluorescent light fixture
    B. electric motor
    C. doorbell circuit
    D. incandescent light fixture

6. Most of the lighting circuits in buildings operate on _____ volts.   6.__
    A. 6   B. 12   C. 120   D. 208

7. An ordinary wall switch called a *silent switch* contains a liquid called   7.__
    A. water   B. mercury   C. oil   D. naptha

8. The rating of the circuit breaker in a lighting circuit is determined by the   8.__

    A. load connected to the circuit
    B. current carrying capacity of the wire
    C. ambient temperature
    D. length of the wire

9. One ADVANTAGE of rubber insulation is that it 9.____

    A. does not deteriorate with age
    B. is able to withstand high temperatures
    C. does not absorb much moisture
    D. is not damaged by oil

10. The SIMPLEST device for interrupting an overloaded electrical circuit is a 10.____

    A. fuse   B. relay
    C. capacitor   D. choke coil

11. Electric service meters are read in 11.____

    A. kilowatt hours   B. electrons
    C. amperes   D. volts

12. The device used to reduce the voltage of an electric circuit is the 12.____

    A. voltmeter   B. fuse
    C. circuit breaker   D. transformer

13. Ordinary light bulbs are USUALLY rated in 13.____

    A. watts   B. ohms   C. amperes   D. filaments

14. The electric plug on a scrubbing machine should be plugged into a 14.____

    A. light socket   B. wall outlet
    C. fuse receptacle   D. dimmer switch

15. The device which should be used to connect the output shaft of an electric motor to the input shaft of a centrifugal pump is the 15.____

    A. flexible coupling   B. petcock
    C. alemite fitting   D. clutch

16. When comparing a 60 watt yellow bulb with a 60 watt clear bulb, it can be said that they BOTH 16.____

    A. give the same amount of light
    B. use the same amount of power
    C. will burn for at least 60 hours
    D. will burn for at least 60 days

17. The output capacity of an electric motor is USUALLY rated in 17.____

    A. kilowatts   B. horsepower
    C. percent   D. cubic feet

18. A fuse will burn out whenever it is subjected to excessive 18.____

    A. resistance   B. voltage
    C. current   D. capacitance

19. The one of the following that is BEST to use to smooth a commutator is 19.____

    A. Number 1/0 emery cloth   B. Number 00 sandpaper
    C. Number 2 steel wool   D. a safe edge file

20. The electric service that is provided to MOST schools in the city is NOMINALLY _____   20._
volt- _____ phase - _____ wire - _____ volts to ground.

    A.   208; 3; 4; 120   B.   208; 3; 3; 208
    C.   220; 2; 3; 110   D.   440; 3; 4; 240

21. All the fuses in an electrical panel are good but the clips on the fuse in circuit No. 1 are   21._
much hotter than the clips of the other fuses.
Of the following, the MOST likely cause of this condition is that

    A.   circuit No. 1 is greatly overloaded
    B.   circuit No. 1 is carrying much less than rated load
    C.   the room temperature is abnormally high
    D.   the fuse in circuit No. 1 is very loose in its clips

22. Before putting two DC engine generators on the line in parallel, it is USUALLY necessary   22._
to

    A.   adjust the speeds so that both are running at exactly the same speed
    B.   adjust the loads so that each machine will take its proportionate share
    C.   adjust the field of the incoming unit
    D.   lower the line voltage

23. Of the following, the BEST type of AC motor to use for direct connection to a timing   23._
device which must be very accurate is a _____ motor.

    A.   synchronous   B.   squirrel cage
    C.   wound rotor   D.   single phase capacitor

24. In running temporary electric wiring for a display requiring the use of 30 incandescent 50-   24._
watt lamps at the usual lighting voltage, the two main 120V loads supplying this load
would carry MOST NEARLY _____ amps.

    A.   23.9   B.   12.5   C.   17.8   D.   9.5

25. The BEST of the following tools to use for cutting off a piece of single conductor #6 rub-   25._
ber insulated lead covered cable is a

    A.   pair of electrician's pliers
    B.   hacksaw
    C.   hammer and cold chisel
    D.   lead knife

KEY (CORRECT ANSWERS)

1.	B		11.	A
2.	C		12.	D
3.	C		13.	A
4.	C		14.	B
5.	A		15.	A
6.	C		16.	B
7.	B		17.	B
8.	B		18.	C
9.	C		19.	B
10.	A		20.	A

21.	D
22.	C
23.	A
24.	B
25.	B

———

TEST 4

DIRECTIONS: Each question or incomplete statement is followed by several suggested answers or completions. Select the one that BEST answers the question or completes the statement. *PRINT THE LETTER OF THE CORRECT ANSWER IN THE SPACE AT THE RIGHT.*

1. An indication that a fluorescent lamp in a fixture should be replaced is   1.___

    A. humming in the fixture
    B. the ends of the lamp remain black when the lamp is lit
    C. poor or slow starting
    D. the lamp does not shut off each time the OFF button is pressed

2. Asbestos is used as a covering on electrical wires to provide protection from   2.___

    A. high voltage   B. high temperatures
    C. water damage   D. electrolysis

3. Many electric power tools, such as drills, have a third conductor in the line cord which   3.___
   should be connected to a grounded part of the power receptacle.
   The reason for this is to

    A. have a spare wire in case one power wire should break
    B. strengthen the power lead so that it cannot be easily damaged
    C. protect the user of the tool from electrical shocks
    D. allow use of the tool for extended periods of time without overheating

4. A riser diagram is an electrical drawing which would give information about the   4.___

    A. voltage drop in feeders
    B. size of feeders and panel loads
    C. external connections to equipment
    D. sequence of operation of devices and equipment

5. An electric motor driven air compressor is automatically started and stopped by a   5.___

    A. thermostat   B. line air valve
    C. pressure switch   D. float trap

6. The term *kilowatt hours* describes the consumption of   6.___

    A. energy   B. radiation
    C. cooling capacity   D. conductance

7. AC voltage may be converted to DC voltage by means of a   7.___

    A. magnet   B. rectifier
    C. voltage regulator   D. transducer

8. The metal which has the GREATEST resistance to the flow of electricity is   8.___

    A. steel   B. copper   C. silver   D. gold

9. Tinning a soldering iron means

    A. applying flux to the tip
    B. cleaning the tip to make it bright
    C. applying a coat of solder to the tip
    D. heating the iron to the proper temperature

10. Electricians working around *live wires* should wear gloves made of

    A. asbestos   B. metal mesh
    C. leather   D. rubber

11.

METER READING AT BEGENNING OF PERIOD

METER READING AT END OF PERIOD

The above are the readings on the electric meter at the beginning and end of a period. The TOTAL kilowatt hour consumption is

    A. 264   B. 570   C. 61   D. 175

12. The modern multiple-circuit program instrument which automatically controls bell signals in a school USUALLY includes

    A. automatic resetting of electric clocks throughout the school
    B. automatic ringing of room bells when the fire bell switch is closed
    C. prevention of manual control of schedules by eliminating manual control switches
    D. provision for automatic cutout of the schedule for any 24-hour day desired

13. Of the following, the device which uses the GREATEST amount of electric power is the

    A. electric typewriter

    B. $\frac{1}{4}$ inch electric drill

    C. floor scrubbing machine
    D. oil burner ignition transformer

14. Meters which indicate the electric power consumed in a public building are read in

    A. kilowatt-hours   B. volts
    C. cubic feet   D. degree days

15. The MAIN reason for grounding the outer shell of an electric fixture is to   15.__

    A. provide additional support for the fixture
    B. reduce the cost of installation of the fixture
    C. provide a terminal to which the wires can be attached
    D. reduce the chance of electric shock

16. The BEST way to determine whether the locknuts on terminals in an electrical terminal   16.__
box have become loose is to

    A. use an electric tester
    B. try to tighten the nuts with an appropriate wrench
    C. tap the nuts with an insulated handle
    D. try to loosen the nuts with a pair of pliers

17. The PROPER flux to use for soldering electric wire connections is   17.__

    A. rosin   B. killed acid
    C. borax   D. zinc chloride

18. A fusestat differs from an ordinary plug fuse in that a fusestat has   18.__

    A. less current carrying capacity
    B. different size threads
    C. an aluminum shell instead of a copper shell
    D. no threads

19. A grounding type 120-volt receptacle differs from an ordinary electric receptacle MAINLY   19.__
in that a grounding receptacle

    A. is larger than the ordinary receptacle
    B. has openings for a three prong plug
    C. can be used for larger machinery
    D. has a built-in circuit breaker

20. In a 110-220 volt three-wire circuit, the neutral wire is USUALLY   20.__

    A. black   B. red   C. white   D. green

21. Brushes on fractional horsepower universal motors are MOST often made of   21.__

    A. flexible copper strands   B. rigid carbon blocks
    C. thin wire strips   D. collector rings

22. A ground wire that is too small is dangerous because it will   22.__

    A. generate heat   B. blow a fuse
    C. increase the voltage   D. increase the current

23. A 115-volt hot water heater has a resistance of 5.75 ohms. The current it will take at   23.__
rated voltage is

    A. 15   B. 20   C. 13   D. 23

24. If a 30 ampere fuse is placed in a fuse box for a circuit requiring a 15 ampere fuse,   24.____

    A.   serious damage to the circuit may result from an overload
    B.   better protection will be provided for the circuit
    C.   the larger fuse will tend to blow more often since it carries more current
    D.   it will eliminate maintenance problems

25. Metal tubing through which electric wires of buildings are run is called   25.____

    A.   insulation   B.   conduit
    C.   duct   D.   sleeve

KEY (CORRECT ANSWERS)

1.	B		11.	D
2.	B		12.	A
3.	C		13.	C
4.	B		14.	A
5.	C		15.	D
6.	A		16.	B
7.	B		17.	A
8.	A		18.	B
9.	C		19.	B
10.	D		20.	C

21. B
22. A
23. B
24. A
25. B

TEST 5

DIRECTIONS: Each question or incomplete statement is followed by several suggested answers or completions. Select the one that BEST answers the question or completes the statement. *PRINT THE LETTER OF THE CORRECT ANSWER IN THE SPACE AT THE RIGHT.*

1. *Found reading* and *left reading* are terms associated with   1.__

   A. petrometers   B. electric meters
   C. gas meters   D. water meters

2. When lamps are wired in parallel, the failure of one lamp will   2.__

   A. break the electric circuit to the other lamps
   B. have no effect on the power supply to the other lamps
   C. increase noticeably the light production of the other lamps
   D. cause excessive current to flow through the other lamps

3. The MAIN objection to using a copper penny in place of a blown fuse is that   3.__

   A. the penny will conduct electric current
   B. the penny will reduce the current flowing in the line
   C. melting of the penny will probably occur
   D. the line will not be protected against excessive current

4. The term *mogul base* is GENERALLY associated with   4.__

   A. boiler compound   B. stock cleaning solution
   C. insecticide   D. lamps

5. When connecting lamp sockets to a lighting circuit, the shell should ALWAYS be con-   5.__
   nected to the white wire of the circuit to

   A. balance the load on the system
   B. reduce the possibility of accidental shock
   C. eliminate blowing the fuse in case the socket becomes grounded
   D. protect the circuit against reverse current

6. The MAIN purpose of periodic inspections and tests of electrical equipment is to   6.__

   A. encourage the workers to take better care of the equipment
   B. familiarize the workers with the equipment
   C. keep the workers busy during otherwise slack periods
   D. discover minor faults before they develop into major faults

7. The current rating of the fuse to use in a lighting circuit is determined by the   7.__

   A. connected load   B. line voltage
   C. capacity of the wiring   D. rating of the switch

8. Artificial respiration after a severe electric shock is ALWAYS necessary when the shock   8.__
   results in

   A. unconsciousness   B. stoppage of breathing
   C. bleeding   D. a burn

9. If you find a co-worker lying unconscious across an electric wire, the FIRST thing you should do is

    A. get him off the wire   B. call the foreman
    C. get a doctor   D. shut off the power

9.____

10. A solenoid valve is actuated by

    A. air pressure   B. electric current
    C. temperature change   D. light rays

10.____

11.

11.____

The electrician's bit is indicated by the number

    A. 1   B. 2   C. 3   D. 4

12. BX is a designation for a type of

    A. flexible armored electric cable
    B. flexible gas line
    C. rigid conduit
    D. electrical insulation

12.____

13. *WYE-WYE* and *DELTA-WYE* are two

    A. types of DC motor windings
    B. arrangements of 3-phase transformer connections
    C. types of electrical splices
    D. shapes of commutator bars

13.____

14. When joining electric wires together in a fixture box, the BEST thing to use are wire

    A. connectors   B. couplings
    C. clamps   D. bolts

14.____

15. If the name plate of a motor indicates that it is a split phase motor, it is LIKELY that this motor   15.___

    A. is a universal motor
    B. operates on DC only
    C. operates on AC only
    D. operates either on DC at full power or on AC at reduced power

16. Rigid steel conduit used for the protection of electrical wiring is GENERALLY either galvanized or enameled both inside and out in order to   16.___

    A. prevent damage to the wire insulation
    B. make threading of the conduit easier
    C. prevent corrosion of the conduit
    D. make the conduit easier to handle

17. If a test lamp does not light when placed in series with a fuse and an appropriate battery, it is a GOOD indication that the fuse   17.___

    A. is open-circuited
    B. is short-circuited
    C. is in operating condition
    D. has zero resistance

18. The process of removing the insulation from a wire is called   18.___

    A. braiding   B. skinning   C. sweating   D. tinning

19. A 10-to-1 step-down transformer has an input of 1 ampere at 120 volts AC. If the losses are negligible, the output of the transformer is _____ volts.   19.___

    A. 1 ampere at 12   B. .1 ampere at 1200
    C. 10 amperes at 12   D. 10 amperes at 120

20. In city schools, wiring for motors or lighting is _____ volt, _____.   20.___

    A. 208-220; 4 wire, 60 cycle
    B. 240-110; 3 wire, 4 phase
    C. 120-208; 3 phase, 4 wire
    D. 160-210; 4 phase, 3 wire

21. When using a voltmeter in testing an electric circuit, the voltmeter should be connected   21.___

    A. across the circuit
    B. in series with the circuit
    C. in parallel or series with the circuit
    D. in series with the active element

22. A kilowatt is _____ watts.   22.___

    A. 500   B. 2,000   C. 1,500   D. 1,000

23. Of the following classifications, the one which pertains to fires in electrical equipment is Class   23.___

    A. A   B. B   C. C   D. D

24. The lighting systems in public buildings usually operate MOST NEARLY on _____ volts.   24._____

    A. 6   B. 24   C. 115   D. 220

25. A type of portable tool used to bend electrical conduit is called a   25._____

    A. helve   B. newel   C. spandrel   D. hickey

KEY (CORRECT ANSWERS)

1.	B		11.	C
2.	B		12.	A
3.	D		13.	B
4.	D		14.	A
5.	B		15.	C
6.	D		16.	C
7.	C		17.	A
8.	B		18.	B
9.	D		19.	C
10.	B		20.	B

21.	A
22.	D
23.	C
24.	C
25.	D

TEST 6

DIRECTIONS: Each question or incomplete statement is followed by several suggested answers or completions. Select the one that BEST answers the question or completes the statement. *PRINT THE LETTER OF THE CORRECT ANSWER IN THE SPACE AT THE RIGHT.*

1. In a 4-wire, 3-phase electrical supply system, the voltage between one phase and ground used for the lighting load is MOST NEARLY

    A. 440   B. 230   C. 208   D. 115

    1.__

2. Of the following, the one that takes the place of a fuse in an electrical circuit is a

    A. transformer   B. circuit breaker
    C. condenser   D. knife switch

    2.__

3. Escutcheons are USUALLY located

    A. on switch plates
    B. on electrical outlets
    C. around pipes, to cover pipe sleeve openings
    D. around armored electric cable going into a gem box

    3.__

4. It is ADVISABLE to remove broken bulbs from light sockets with

    A. a wooden or hard rubber wedge
    B. pliers
    C. a hammer and chisel
    D. a fuse puller

    4.__

5. A 3-ohm resistor placed across a 12-volt battery will dissipate _____ watts.

    A. 3   B. 4   C. 12   D. 48

    5.__

6. Instead of using fuses, modern electric wiring uses

    A. quick switches   B. circuit breakers
    C. fusible links   D. lag blocks

    6.__

7. In order to reverse the direction of rotation of a series motor, the

    A. connections to the armature should be reversed
    B. connections to both the armature and the series field should be reversed
    C. connections of the motor to the power lines should be reversed
    D. series field should be placed in shunt with the armature

    7.__

8. The BEST flux to use when soldering copper wires in an electric circuit is

    A. sal ammoniac   B. zinc chloride
    C. rosin   D. borax

    8.__

9. A megger is an instrument used to measure

    A. capacitance   B. insulation resistance
    C. power   D. illumination levels

    9.__

10. An electrical drawing is drawn to a scale of 1/4" = 1'.
    If a length of conduit on the drawing measures 7 3/8", the actual length of the conduit, in feet, is MOST NEARLY

    10.____

    A. 7.5'   B. 15.5'   C. 22.5'   D. 29.5'

11. Standard 120-volt plug-type fuses are GENERALLY rated in

    11.____

    A. farads   B. ohms   C. watts   D. amperes

12. Standard 120-volt electric light bulbs are GENERALLY rated in

    12.____

    A. farads   B. ohms   C. watts   D. amperes

13. Of the following colors of electrical conductor coverings, the one which indicates a conductor used SOLELY for grounding portable or fixed electrical equipment is

    13.____

    A. blue   B. green   C. red   D. black

14. A device that operates to vary the resistance of an electrical circuit is USUALLY part of a _____ pressuretrol.

    14.____

    A. high-limit   B. low-limit
    C. manual-reset   D. modulating

15. The type of screwdriver SPECIALLY made to be used in tight spots is the

    15.____

    A. Phillips   B. offset
    C. square shank   D. truss

16. On a plan, the symbol shown at the right USUALLY represents a(n)

    16.____

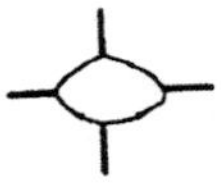

    A. duplex receptacle
    B. electric switch
    C. ceiling outlet
    D. pull box

17. Electric power is measured in

    17.____

    A. volts   B. amperes   C. watts   D. ohms

18. Of the following sizes of copper conductors, the one which has the LEAST current-carrying capacity is _____ AWG.

    18.____

    A. 000   B. 0   C. 8   D. 12

19. When excess current flows, a circuit breaker is opened directly by the action of a

    19.____

    A. condenser   B. transistor
    C. relay   D. solenoid

20. Conduit is used in electrical wiring in order to the wires.

    20.____

    A. waterproof   B. color code
    C. protect   D. insulate

KEY (CORRECT ANSWERS)

1.	D		11.	D
2.	B		12.	C
3.	D		13.	B
4.	A		14.	D
5.	B		15.	B
6.	B		16.	C
7.	A		17.	C
8.	C		18.	D
9.	B		19.	D
10.	D		20.	C

SAFETY
EXAMINATION SECTION
TEST 1

DIRECTIONS: Each question or incomplete statement is followed by several suggested answers or completions. Select the one that BEST answers the question or completes the statement. *PRINT THE LETTER OF THE CORRECT ANSWER IN THE SPACE AT THE RIGHT.*

1. The type of portable fire extinguisher which is *particularly* suited for extinguishing flammable liquid fires is the

    A. soda-acid type
    C. pump tank type
    B. foam type
    D. loaded stream type

1.____

2. The extinguishing agent in a soda-acid fire extinguisher is

    A. water
    C. sodium bicarbonate
    B. hydrochloric acid
    D. carbon dioxide

2.____

3. The MAIN reason for not permitting more than one person to work on a ladder at the same time is that

    A. the ladder might get overloaded
    B. several persons on the ladder might obstruct each other
    C. time would be lost going up and down the ladder
    D. several persons could not all face the ladder at one time

3.____

4. Safety on the job is BEST assured by

    A. keeping alert
    B. working only with new tools
    C. working very slowly
    D. avoiding the necessity for working overtime

4.____

5. A serious safety hazard occurs when a

    A. hardened steel hammer is used to strike a hardened steel surface
    B. soft iron hammer is used to strike a hardened steel surface
    C. hardened steel hammer is used to strike a soft iron surface
    D. soft iron hammer is used to strike a soft iron surface

5.____

6. Protective goggles should NOT be worn when

    A. standing on a ladder drilling a steel beam
    B. descending a ladder after completing a job
    C. chipping concrete near a third rail
    D. sharpening a cold chisel on a grinding stone

6.____

7. In an accident report, the information which may be MOST useful in DECREASING the recurrence of similar type accidents is the

    A. extent of injuries sustained
    B. time the accident happened
    C. number of people involved
    D. cause of the accident

7.___

8. A laborer was sent upstairs to get a 20-pound sack of rock salt. While going downstairs and reading the printing on the sack, he fell and the sack of rock salt fell and broke his toe.
    Which of the following is *most likely* to have been the most important cause of the accident? The

    A. stairs were beginning to become worn
    B. laborer was carrying too heavy a sack of rock salt
    C. rock salt was in a place that was too inaccessible
    D. laborer was not careful about the way he went down the stairs

8.___

9. Shoes which have a sponge rubber sole should NOT be worn around a work area because such a sole

    A. will wear quickly
    B. is not waterproof
    C. does not keep the feet warm
    D. is easily punctured by steel objects

9.___

10. Gloves should be used when handling

    A. lanterns   B. wooden rules
    C. heavy ropes   D. all small tools

10.___

11. Steel helmets give workers the MOST protection from

    A. falling objects   B. eye injuries
    C. fire   D. electric shock

11.___

12. It is POOR practice to wear goggles when

    A. chipping stone
    B. using a grinder
    C. climbing or descending ladders
    D. handling molten metal

12.___

13. In construction work, *almost all* accidents can be blamed on the

    A. failure of an individual to give close attention to the job assigned to him
    B. use of improper tools
    C. lack of cooperation among the men in a gang
    D. fact that an incompetent man was placed in a key position

13.___

14. If it is necessary for you to do some work with your hands under a piece of heavy equip-   14.____
    ment, while a fellow worker lifts up and holds one end of it by means of a pinch bar, one
    IMPORTANT precaution you should take is to

    A. wear gloves
    B. watch the bar to be ready if it slips
    C. insert a temporary block to support the piece
    D. work as fast as possible

15. The MOST important safety precaution to follow when using an electric drill press is to   15.____

    A. wear safety shoes
    B. drill at a slow speed
    C. use plenty of cutting oil
    D. clamp the work firmly

16. Assume that the top of a 12-foot portable straight ladder is placed against a wall but is   16.____
    not held by a man or fastened in any way. In order to be safe, the ladder should be placed
    so that the distance from the wall to the foot of the ladder is

    A. not over 3 feet   B. not over 4 feet
    C. at least 4 feet   D. at least 5 feet

17. A good safety rule to follow is that water should NOT be used to extinguish fires in or   17.____
    around electrical apparatus. Of the following, the PRIMARY reason for this is that water

    A. will damage the insulation
    B. will corrode the electrical conductors
    C. may cause the circuit fuse to blow
    D. may conduct electric current and cause a shock hazard

18. One should be extremely careful to keep open flames and sparks away from storage bat-   18.____
    teries when they are being charged because the

    A. sulphate given off during this operation is highly flammable
    B. hydrogen given off during this operation is highly flammable
    C. oxygen given off during this operation is extremely flammable
    D. static electricity of the battery may cause combustion

19. A good safety rule to follow is that an electric hand tool, such as a portable electric drill,   19.____
    should never be lifted or carried by its service cord. Of the following, the PRIMARY rea-
    son for this rule is that the

    A. tool might swing and be damaged by striking some hard object
    B. cord might be pulled off its terminals and become short circuited
    C. tool may slip out of the hand as it is hard to get a good grip on a slick rubber cord
    D. rubber covering of the cord might overstretch

20. When a man is working on a 15-foot ladder with its top placed against a wall, the MAXI-   20.____
    MUM safe distance that he may reach out to one side of the ladder is

    A. as far out as he can reach lifting one foot off the rung for balance
    B. as far out as he can reach without bending his body more than 45 from the vertical
    C. one third the length of the ladder
    D. as far out as his arm's length

21. When NOT in use, oily waste rags should be stored in

    A. water-tight oak barrels
    B. open metal containers
    C. sealed cardboard boxes
    D. self-closing, metal containers

21.___

Questions 22-25.

DIRECTIONS: Each question consists of a statement. You are to indicate whether the statement is TRUE (T) or FALSE (F). *PRINT THE LETTER OF THE CORRECT ANSWER IN THE SPACE AT THE RIGHT.*

22. To help prevent accidents, gloves should be worn when handling rough wood or broken glass.

22.___

23. The safest and quickest way to remove a burnt-out light bulb from a ceiling fixture is to stand on a chair on top of a desk or table.

23.___

24. You should get help before lifting a large or heavy object which you believe is beyond your strength.

24.___

25. In lifting a heavy object, keep your feet together and never crouch down.

25.___

KEY (CORRECT ANSWERS)

1.	B		11.	A
2.	A		12.	C
3.	A		13.	A
4.	A		14.	C
5.	A		15.	D
6.	B		16.	A
7.	D		17.	D
8.	D		18.	B
9.	D		19.	B
10.	C		20.	D

21.	D
22.	T
23.	F
24.	T
25.	F

TEST 2

DIRECTIONS: Each question or incomplete statement is followed by several suggested answers or completions. Select the one that BEST answers the question or completes the statement. *PRINT THE LETTER OF THE CORRECT ANSWER IN THE SPACE AT THE RIGHT.*

1. Safety on any job is BEST assured by

   1._____

   A. working very slowly
   B. following every rule
   C. never working alone
   D. keeping alert

2. Of the following firefighting agents used in portable fire extinguishers, the one which is *most likely* to spread a flammable liquid fire is

   2._____

   A. foam
   C. carbon dioxide
   B. a solid stream of water
   D. dry chemical

3. Transit employees are cautioned, as a safety measure, not to use water to extinguish fires involving electrical equipment. One logical reason for this caution is that the water

   3._____

   A. will cause harmful steam
   B. will not extinguish a fire started by electricity
   C. may transmit electrical shock to the user
   D. may crack hot insulators

4. When carrying pipe, employees are cautioned against lifting with the fingers inserted in the ends. The *probable* reason for this caution is to avoid the possibility of

   4._____

   A. dropping and damaging pipe
   B. getting dirt and perspiration on inside of pipe
   C. cutting the fingers on edge of pipe
   D. straining finger muscles

5. The MOST common cause for a workman to lose his balance and fall when working from an extension ladder is

   5._____

   A. too much spring in the ladder
   B. sideways sliding of the top
   C. exerting a heavy pull on an object which gives suddenly
   D. working on something directly behind the ladder

6. Protective goggles SHOULD be worn when

   6._____

   A. climbing a ladder
   C. using a chipping hammer
   B. reading a gage
   D. driving a hi-lo truck

7. An employee will *most likely* avoid accidental injury if he

   7._____

   A. stops to rest frequently
   C. keeps mentally alert
   B. works alone
   D. works very slowly

8. Electrical helpers on the subway system are instructed in the use of fire extinguishers. The *probable* reason for including helpers in this instruction is that the helper

    A. cannot do the more important work
    B. may be the cause of a fire because of his inexperience
    C. may be alone when a fire starts
    D. will become interested in fire prevention

8._

9. There are a few workers who are seemingly prone to accidents and who, regardless of their assigned job, have a higher accident rate than the average worker. If your co-worker is known to be such an individual, the BEST course for you to pursue would be to

    A. do most of the assigned work yourself
    B. refuse to work with this individual
    C. provide him with a copy of all rules and regulations
    D. personally check all safety precautions on each job

9._

10. A rule of the transit system states that, "In walking on the track, walk opposite the direction of traffic on that track if possible." By logical reasoning, the *principal* safety idea behind this rule is that the man on the track

    A. is more likely to see an approaching train
    B. will be seen more readily by the motorman
    C. need not be as careful
    D. is better able to judge the speed of the train

10._

11. Of the following types of fire extinguishers, the one that should NOT be used to extinguish a burning gasoline fire is

    A. soda acid   B. dry chemical
    C. carbon dioxide   D. liquified gas

11._

12. It is NOT necessary to wear protective goggles when

    A. drilling rivet holes in a steel beam
    B. sharpening tools on a power grinder
    C. welding a steel plate to a pipe column
    D. laying up a cinder block partition

12._

13. The MOST important reason for insisting on neatness in maintenance quarters is that it

    A. increases the available storage space
    B. makes for good employee morale
    C. prevents tools from becoming rusty
    D. decreases the chances of accidents to employees

13._

14. There are many steel ladders and stairways installed in the subway for the use of transit workers. Their GREATEST danger is that they

    A. have sharp edges causing cuts
    B. are slippery when greasy and wet
    C. cause colds
    D. have no "give" and thus cause fatigue

14._

15. Of the following, the MOST common result of accidents occurring while using hand tools is   15.____

    A. loss of limbs   B. loss of eyesight
    C. infection of wounds   D. loss of life

16. The one of the following extinguishing agents which should NOT be used on an oil fire is   16.____

    A. foam   B. sand
    C. water   D. carbon dioxide

17. The extinguishing agent in a portable sodaacid fire extinguisher is   17.____

    A. sodium bicarbonate   B. sulphuric acid
    C. carbon dioxide   D. water

18. A foam-type fire extinguisher extinguishes fires by   18.____

    A. cooling only   B. drenching only
    C. smothering only   D. cooling and smothering

19. The extinguishing agent in a soda-acid fire extinguisher is   19.____

    A. carbon dioxide
    B. water
    C. carbon tetrachloride
    D. calcium chloride solution

20. The proper extinguisher to use on an electrical fire in an operating electric motor is   20.____

    A. foam   B. carbon dioxide
    C. soda and acid   D. water

21. Transit workers are advised to report injuries caused by nails, no matter how slight. The MOST important reason for this rule is that this type of injury   21.____

    A. is caused by violating safety rules
    B. can only be caused by carelessness
    C. generally causes dangerous bleeding
    D. may result in a serious condition

Questions 22-25.

DIRECTIONS: Each question consists of a statement. You are to indicate whether the statement is TRUE (T) or FALSE (F). *PRINT THE LETTER OF THE CORRECT ANSWER IN THE SPACE AT THE RIGHT.*

22. The soda-and-acid type of extinguisher is effective for use on a flammable liquid fire.   22.____

23. The carbon dioxide type of extinguisher is suitable for use on electrical fires.   23.____

24. For good maintenance, the pressure cartridge in a cartridge-operated extinguisher should be replaced if the weight is 1/2 ounce less than is stamped on the cartridge.   24.____

25. A paper fire is considered a Class A fire.   25.____

KEY (CORRECT ANSWERS)

1.	D		11.	A
2.	B		12.	D
3.	C		13.	D
4.	C		14.	B
5.	C		15.	C
6.	C		16.	C
7.	C		17.	D
8.	C		18.	D
9.	D		19.	B
10.	A		20.	B

21.	D
22.	F
23.	T
24.	T
25.	T

READING COMPREHENSION
UNDERSTANDING AND INTERPRETING WRITTEN MATERIAL
EXAMINATION SECTION
TEST 1

DIRECTIONS   Each question or incomplete statement is followed by several suggested answers or completions. Select the one that BEST answers the question or completes the statement. *PRINT THE LETTER OF THE CORRECT ANSWER IN THE SPACE AT THE RIGHT.*

Questions 1-8.

DIRECTIONS: Questions 1 through 8 are to be answered on the basis of the following regulations governing Newspaper Carriers when on subway trains or station platforms. These Newspaper Carriers are issued badges which entitle them to enter subway stations, when carrying papers in accordance with these regulations, without paying a fare.

REGULATIONS GOVERNING NEWSPAPER CARRIERS WHEN ON SUBWAY TRAINS OR STATION PLATFORMS

1. Carriers must wear badges at all times when on trains.
2. Carriers must not sort, separate, or wrap bundles on trains or insert sections.
3. Carriers must not obstruct platform of cars or stations.
4. Carriers may make delivery to stands inside the stations by depositing their badge with the station agent.
5. Throwing of bundles is strictly prohibited and will be cause for arrest.
6. Each bundle must not be over 18" x 12" x 15".
7. Not more than two bundles shall be carried by each carrier. (An extra fare to be charged for a second bundle.)
8. No wire to be used on bundles carried into stations.

1. These regulations do NOT prohibit carriers on trains from _____ newspapers.   1.____

   A. sorting bundles of   B. carrying bundles of
   C. wrapping bundles of   D. inserting sections into

2. A carrier delivering newspapers to a stand inside of the station MUST   2.____

   A. wear his badge at all times
   B. leave his badge with the railroad clerk
   C. show his badge to the railroad clerk
   D. show his badge at the newsstand

3. Carriers are warned against throwing bundles of newspapers from trains MAINLY because these acts may   3.____

   A. wreck the stand   B. cause injury to passengers
   C. hurt the carrier   D. damage the newspaper

4. It is permissible for a carrier to temporarily leave his bundles of newspapers   4._____

    A. near the subway car's door
    B. at the foot of the station stairs
    C. in front of the exit gate
    D. on a station bench

5. Of the following, the carrier who should NOT be restricted from entering the subway is   5._____
the one carrying a bundle which is _____long, _____ wide, and _____ high.

    A. 15"; 18"; 18"   B. 18"; 12"; 18"
    C. 18"; 12"; 15"   D. 18"; 15"; 15"

6. A carrier who will have to pay one fare is carrying _____ bundle(s).   6._____

    A. one   B. two   C. three   D. four

7. Wire may NOT be used for tying bundles because it may be   7._____

    A. rusty
    B. expensive
    C. needed for other purposes
    D. dangerous to other passengers

8. If a carrier is arrested in violation of these regulations, the PROBABLE reason is that he   8._____

    A. carried too many papers
    B. was not wearing his badge
    C. separated bundles of newspapers on the train
    D. tossed a bundle of newspapers to a carrier on a train

Questions 9-12.

DIRECTIONS: Questions 9 through 12 are to be answered on the basis of the Bulletin printed below. Read this Bulletin carefully before answering these questions. Select your answers ONLY on the basis of this Bulletin.

BULLETIN

Rule 107(m) states, in part, that *Before closing doors they (Conductors) must afford passengers an opportunity to detrain and entrain...*

Doors must be left open long enough to allow passengers to enter and exit from the train. Closing doors on passengers too quickly does not help to shorten the station stop and is a violation of the safety and courtesy which must be accorded to all our passengers.

The proper and effective way to keep passengers moving in and out of the train is to use the public address system. When the train is excessively crowded and passengers on the platform are pushing those in the cars, it may be necessary to close the doors after a reasonable period of time has been allowed.

Closing doors on passengers too quickly is a violation of rules and will be cause for disciplinary actions.

9. Which of the following statements is CORRECT about closing doors on passengers too quickly? It

    A. will shorten the running time from terminal to terminal
    B. shortens the station stop but is a violation of safety and courtesy
    C. does not help shorten the station stop time
    D. makes the passengers detrain and entrain quicker

10. The BEST way to get passengers to move in and out of cars quickly is to

    A. have the platform conductors urge passengers to move into doorways
    B. make announcements over the public address system
    C. start closing doors while passengers are getting on
    D. set a fixed time for stopping at each station

11. The conductor should leave doors open at each station stop long enough for passengers to

    A. squeeze into an excessively crowded train
    B. get from the local to the express train
    C. get off and get on the train
    D. hear the announcements over the public address system

12. Closing doors on passengers too quickly is a violation of rules and is cause for

    A. the conductor's immediate suspension
    B. the conductor to be sent back to the terminal for another assignment
    C. removal of the conductor at the next station
    D. disciplinary action to be taken against the conductor

Questions 13-15.

DIRECTIONS: Questions 13 through 15 are to be answered on the basis of the Bulletin printed below. Read this Bulletin carefully before answering these questions. Select your answers ONLY on the basis of this Bulletin.

BULLETIN

Conductors assigned to train service are not required to wear uniform caps from June 1 to September 30, inclusive.

Conductors assigned to platform duty are required to wear the uniform cap at all times. Conductors are reminded that they must furnish their badge numbers to anyone who requests same.

During the above-mentioned period, conductors may remove their uniform coats. The regulation summer short-sleeved shirts must be worn with the regulation uniform trousers. Suspenders are not permitted if the uniform coat is removed. Shoes are to be black but sandals, sneakers, suede, canvas, or two-tone footwear must not be worn.

Conductors may work without uniform tie if the uniform coat is removed. However, only the top collar button may be opened. The tie may not be removed if the uniform coat is worn.

13. Conductors assigned to platform duty are required to wear uniform caps 13.____

  A. at all times except from June 1 to September 30, inclusive
  B. whenever they are on duty
  C. only from June 1 to September 30, inclusive
  D. only when they remove their uniform coats

14. Suspenders are permitted ONLY if conductors wear 14.____

  A. summer short-sleeved shirts with uniform trousers
  B. uniform trousers without belt loops
  C. the type permitted by the authority
  D. uniform coats

15. A conductor MUST furnish his badge number to 15.____

  A. authority supervisors only
  B. members of special inspection only
  C. anyone who asks him for it
  D. passengers only

Questions 16-17.

DIRECTIONS: Questions 16 and 17 are to be answered SOLELY on the basis of the following Bulletin.

BULLETIN

 Effective immediately, Conductors on trains equipped with public address systems shall make the following announcements in addition to their regular station announcement. At stations where passengers normally board trains from their homes or places of employment, the announcement shall be *Good Morning* or *Good Afternoon* or *Good Evening,* depending on the time of the day. At stations where passengers normally leave trains for their homes or places of employment, the announcement shall be *Have a Good Day* or *Good Night,* depending on the time of day or night.

16. The MAIN purpose of making the additional announcements mentioned in the Bulletin is MOST likely to 16.____

  A. keep passengers informed about the time of day
  B. determine whether the public address system works in case of an emergency
  C. make the passengers' ride more pleasant
  D. have the conductor get used to using the public address system

17. According to this Bulletin, a conductor should greet passengers boarding the *D* train at the Coney Island Station at 8 A.M. Monday by announcing 17.____

  A. Have a Good Day
  B. Good Morning
  C. Watch your step as you leave
  D. Good Evening

Questions 18-25.

DIRECTIONS: Questions 18 through 25 are to be answered on the basis of the information regarding the incident given below. Read this information carefully before answering these questions.

INCIDENT

As John Brown, a cleaner, was sweeping the subway station platform, in accordance with his assigned schedule, he was accused by Henry Adams of unnecessarily bumping him with the broom and scolded for doing this work when so many passengers were on the platform. Adams obtained Brown's badge number and stated that he would report the matter to the Transit Authority. Standing around and watching this were Mary Smith, a schoolteacher, Ann Jones, a student, and Joe Black, a maintainer, with Jim Roe, his helper, who had been working on one of the turnstiles. Brown thereupon proceeded to take the names and addresses of these people as required by the Transit Authority rule which directs that names and addresses of as many disinterested witnesses be taken as possible. Shortly thereafter, a train arrived at the station and Adams, as well as several other people, boarded the train and left. Brown went back to his work of sweeping the station.

18.   The cleaner was sweeping the station at this time because

    A.   the platform was unusually dirty
    B.   there were very few passengers on the platform
    C.   he had no regard for the passengers
    D.   it was set by his work schedule

18.____

19.   This incident proves that

    A.   witnesses are needed in such cases
    B.   porters are generally careless
    C.   subway employees stick together
    D.   brooms are dangerous in the subway

19.____

20.   Joe Black was a

    A.   helper
    C.   cleaner
    B.   maintainer
    D.   teacher

20.____

21.   The number of persons witnessing this incident was

    A.   2   B.   3   C.   4   D.   5

21.____

22.   The addresses of witnesses are required so that they may later be

    A.   depended on to testify
    C.   paid
    B.   recognized
    D.   located

22.____

23.   The person who said he would report this incident to the transit authority was

    A.   Black   B.   Adams   C.   Brown   D.   Roe

23.____

24. The ONLY person of the following who positively did NOT board the train was   24.____

    A. Brown   B. Smith   C. Adams   D. Jones

25. As a result of this incident,   25.____

    A. no action need be taken against the cleaner unless Adams makes a written complaint
    B. the cleaner should be given the rest of the day off
    C. the handles of the brooms used should be made shorter
    D. Brown's badge number should be changed

KEY (CORRECT ANSWERS)

1.	B	11.	C
2.	B	12.	D
3.	B	13.	B
4.	D	14.	D
5.	C	15.	C
6.	A	16.	C
7.	D	17.	B
8.	D	18.	D
9.	C	19.	A
10.	B	20.	B

21.	C
22.	D
23.	B
24.	A
25.	A

TEST 2

DIRECTIONS: Each question or incomplete statement is followed by several suggested answers or completions. Select the one that BEST answers the question or completes the statement. *PRINT THE LETTER OF THE CORRECT ANSWER IN THE SPACE AT THE RIGHT.*

Questions 1-10.

DIRECTIONS: Questions 1 through 10 are to be answered on the basis of the information contained in the following safety rules. Read the rules carefully before answering these questions.

SAFETY RULES

Employees must take every precaution to prevent accidents, or injury to persons, or damage to property. For this reason, they must observe conditions of the equipment and tools with which they work, and the structures upon which they work.

It is the duty of all employees to report to their superior all dangerous conditions which they may observe. Employees must use every precaution to prevent the origin of fire. If they discover smoke or a fire in the subway, they shall proceed to the nearest telephone and notify the trainmaster giving their name, badge number, and location of the trouble.

In case of accidents on the subway system, employees must, if possible, secure the name, address, and telephone number of any passengers who may have been injured.

Employees at or near the location of trouble on the subway system, whether it be a fire or an accident, shall render all practical assistance which they are qualified to perform.

1. The BEST way for employees to prevent an accident is to   1.____

    A. secure the names of the injured persons
    B. arrive promptly at the location of the accident
    C. give their name and badge numbers to the trainmaster
    D. take all necessary precautions

2. In case of trouble, trackmen are NOT expected to   2.____

    A. report fires
    B. give help if they don't know how
    C. secure telephone numbers of persons injured in subway accidents
    D. give their badge number to anyone

3. Trackmen MUST   3.____

    A. be present at all fires
    B. see all accidents
    C. report dangerous conditions
    D. be the first to discover smoke in the subway

4. Observing conditions means to
    A. look at things carefully
    B. report what you see
    C. ignore things that are none of your business
    D. correct dangerous conditions

4.____

5. A dangerous condition existing on the subway system which a trackman should observe and report to his superior would be
    A. passengers crowding into trains
    B. trains running behind schedule
    C. tools in defective condition
    D. some newspapers on the track

5.____

6. If a trackman discovers a badly worn rail, he should
    A. not take any action
    B. remove the worn section of rail
    C. notify his superior
    D. replace the rail

6.____

7. The MAIN reason a trackman should observe the condition of his tools is
    A. so that they won't be stolen
    B. because they don't belong to him
    C. to prevent accidents
    D. because they cannot be replaced

7.____

8. If a passenger who paid his fare is injured in a subway accident, it is MOST important that an employee obtain the passenger's
    A. name   B. age
    C. badge number   D. destination

8.____

9. An employee who happens to be at the scene of an accident on a crowded station of the system should
    A. not give assistance unless he chooses to do so
    B. leave the scene immediately
    C. question all bystanders
    D. render whatever assistance he can

9.____

10. If a trackman discovers a fire at one end of a station platform and telephones the information to the trainmaster, he need NOT give
    A. the trainmaster's name
    B. the name of the station involved
    C. his own name
    D. the number of his badge

10.____

Questions 11-15.

DIRECTIONS: Questions 11 through 15 are to be answered on the basis of the information contained in the safety regulations given below. Refer to these rules in answering these questions.

REGULATIONS FOR SMALL GROUPS WHO MOVE FROM POINT TO POINT ON THE TRACKS

Employees who perform duties on the tracks in small groups and who move from point to point along the trainway must be on the alert at all times and prepared to clear the track when a train approaches without unnecessarily slowing it down. Underground at all times, and out-of-doors between sunset and sunrise, such employees must not enter upon the tracks unless each of them is equipped with an approved light. Flashlights must not be used for protection by such groups. Upon clearing the track to permit a train to pass, each member of the group must give a proceed signal, by hand or light, to the motorman of the train. Whenever such small groups are working in an area protected by caution lights or flags, but are not members of the gang for whom the flagging protection was established, they must not give proceed signals to motormen. The purpose of this rule is to avoid a motorman's confusing such signal with that of the flagman who is protecting a gang. Whenever a small group is engaged in work of an engrossing nature or at any time when the view of approaching trains is limited by reason of curves or otherwise, one man of the group, equipped with a whistle, must be assigned properly to warn and protect the man or men at work and must not perform any other duties while so assigned.

11.   If a small group of men are traveling along the tracks toward their work location and a train approaches, they should

    A.   stop the train
    B.   signal the motorman to go slowly
    C.   clear the track
    D.   stop immediately

11._____

12.   Small groups may enter upon the tracks

    A.   only between sunset and sunrise
    B.   provided each has an approved light
    C.   provided their foreman has a good flashlight
    D.   provided each man has an approved flashlight

12._____

13.   After a small group has cleared the tracks in an area unprotected by caution lights or flags,

    A.   each member must give the proceed signal to the motorman
    B.   the foreman signals the motorman to proceed
    C.   the motorman can proceed provided he goes slowly
    D.   the last member off the tracks gives the signal to the motorman

13._____

14.   If a small group is working in an area protected by the signals of a track gang, the members of the small group

    A.   need not be concerned with train movement
    B.   must give the proceed signal together with the track gang

14._____

C. can delegate one of their members to give the proceed signal
D. must not give the proceed signal

15. If the view of approaching trains is blocked, the small group should

    A. move to where they can see the trains
    B. delegate one of the group to warn and protect them
    C. keep their ears alert for approaching trains
    D. refuse to work at such locations

15._____

Questions 16-25.

DIRECTIONS: Questions 16 through 25 are to be answered SOLELY on the basis of the article about general safety precautions given below.

GENERAL SAFETY PRECAUTIONS

When work is being done on or next to a track on which regular trains are running, special signals must be displayed as called for in the general rules for flagging. Yellow caution signals, green clear signals, and a flagman with a red danger signal are required for the protection of traffic and workmen in accordance with the standard flagging rules. The flagman shall also carry a white signal for display to the motorman when he may proceed. The foreman in charge must see that proper signals are displayed.

On elevated lines during daylight hours, the yellow signal shall be a yellow flag, the red signal shall be a red flag, the green signal shall be a green flag, and the white signal shall be a white flag. In subway sections, and on elevated lines after dark, the yellow signal shall be a yellow lantern, the red signal shall be a red lantern, the green signal shall be a green lantern, and the white signal shall be a white lantern.

Caution and clear signals are to be secured to the elevated or subway structure with non-metallic fastenings outside the clearance line of the train and on the motorman's side of the track.

16. On elevated lines during daylight hours, the caution signal is a

    A. yellow lantern   B. green lantern
    C. yellow flag   D. green flag

16._____

17. In subway sections, the clear signal is a

    A. yellow lantern   B. green lantern
    C. yellow flag   D. green flag

17._____

18. The MINIMUM number of lanterns that a subway track flagman should carry is

    A. 1   B. 2   C. 3   D. 4

18._____

19. The PRIMARY purpose of flagging is to protect the

    A. flagman   B. motorman
    C. track workers   D. railroad

19._____

20. A suitable fastening for securing caution lights to the elevated or subway structure is   20.____

   A. copper nails   B. steel wire
   C. brass rods   D. cotton twine

21. On elevated structures during daylight hours, the red flag is held by the   21.____

   A. motorman   B. foreman   C. trackman   D. flagman

22. The signal used in the subway to notify a motorman to proceed is a   22.____

   A. white lantern   B. green lantern
   C. red flag   D. yellow flag

23. The caution, clear, and danger signals are displayed for the information of   23.____

   A. trackmen   B. workmen   C. flagmen   D. motormen

24. Since the motorman's cab is on the right-hand side, caution signals should be secured to   24.____
the

   A. right-hand running rail
   B. left-hand running rail
   C. structure to the right of the track
   D. structure to the left of the track

25. In a track work gang, the person responsible for the proper display of signals is the   25.____

   A. track worker   B. foreman
   C. motorman   D. flagman

KEY (CORRECT ANSWERS)

1.	D	11.	C
2.	B	12.	B
3.	C	13.	A
4.	A	14.	D
5.	C	15.	B
6.	C	16.	C
7.	C	17.	B
8.	A	18.	B
9.	D	19.	C
10.	A	20.	D

21.	D
22.	A
23.	D
24.	C
25.	B

TEST 3

DIRECTIONS: Each question or incomplete statement is followed by several suggested answers or completions. Select the one that BEST answers the question or completes the statement. *PRINT THE LETTER OF THE CORRECT ANSWER IN THE SPACE AT THE RIGHT.*

Questions 1-6.

DIRECTIONS: Questions 1 through 6 are to be answered on the basis of the Bulletin Order given below. Refer to this bulletin when answering these questions.

<u>BULLETIN ORDER NO. 67</u>

SUBJECT: Procedure for Handling Fire Occurrences

In order that the Fire Department may be notified of all fires, even those that have been extinguished by our own employees, any employee having knowledge of a fire must notify the Station Department Office immediately on telephone extensions D-4177, D-4181, D-4185, or D-4189.

Specific information regarding the fire should include the location of the fire, the approximate distance north or south of the nearest station, and the track designation, line, and division.

In addition, the report should contain information as to the status of the fire and whether our forces have extinguished it or if Fire Department equipment is required.

When all information has been obtained, the Station Supervisor in Charge in the Station Department Office will notify the Desk Trainmaster of the Division involved.

Richard Roe,
Superintendent

1. An employee having knowledge of a fire should FIRST notify the   1.___

    A. Station Department Office
    B. Fire Department
    C. Desk Trainmaster
    D. Station Supervisor

2. If bulletin order number 1 was issued on January 2, bulletins are being issued at the   2.___
   monthly average of

    A. 8   B. 10   C. 12   D. 14

3. It is clear from the bulletin that   3.___

    A. employees are expected to be expert fire fighters
    B. many fires occur on the transit system
    C. train service is usually suspended whenever a fire occurs
    D. some fires are extinguished without the help of the Fire Department

4. From the information furnished in this bulletin, it can be assumed that the   4.____

    A. Station Department office handles a considerable number of telephone calls
    B. Superintendent Investigates the handling of all subway fires
    C. Fire Department is notified only in ease of large fires
    D. employee first having knowledge of the fire must call all 4 extensions

5. The PROBABLE reason for notifying the Fire Department even when the fire has been   5.____
extinguished by a subway employee is because the Fire Department is

    A. a city agency
    B. still responsible to check the fire
    C. concerned with fire prevention
    D. required to clean up after the fire

6. Information about the fire NOT specifically required is   6.____

    A. track   B. time of day   C. station   D. division

Questions 7-10.

DIRECTIONS: Questions 7 through 10 are to be answered on the basis of the paragraph on fire fighting shown below. When answering these questions, refer to this paragraph.

FIRE FIGHTING

A security officer should remember the cardinal rule that water or soda acid fire extinguishers should not be used on any electrical fire, and apply it in the case of a fire near the third rail. In addition, security officers should familiarize themselves with all available fire alarms and fire-fighting equipment within their assigned posts. Use of the fire alarm should bring responding Fire Department apparatus quickly to the scene. Familiarity with the fire-fighting equipment near his post would help in putting out incipient fires. Any man calling for the Fire Department should remain outside so that he can direct the Fire Department to the fire. As soon as possible thereafter, the special inspection desk must be notified, and a complete written report of the fire, no matter how small, must be submitted to this office. The security officer must give the exact time and place it started, who discovered it, how it was extinguished, the damage done, cause of same, list of any injured persons with the extent of their injuries, and the name of the Fire Chief in charge. All defects noticed by the security officer concerning the fire alarm or any fire-fighting equipment must be reported to the special inspection department.

7. It would be PROPER to use water to put out a fire in a(n)   7.____

    A. electric motor   B. electric switch box
    C. waste paper trash can   D. electric generator

8. After calling the Fire Department from a street box to report a fire, the security officer should then   8.____

    A. return to the fire and help put it out
    B. stay outside and direct the Fire Department to the fire
    C. find a phone and call his boss
    D. write out a report for the special inspection desk

9. A security officer is required to submit a complete written report of a fire   9.____

    A. two weeks after the fire
    B. the day following the fire
    C. as soon as possible
    D. at his convenience

10. In his report of a fire, it is NOT necessary for the security officer to state   10.____

    A. time and place of the fire
    B. who discovered the fire
    C. the names of persons injured
    D. quantity of Fire Department equipment used

Questions 11-16.

DIRECTIONS: Questions 11 through 16 are to be answered on the basis of the Notice given below. Refer to this Notice in answering these questions.

NOTICE

Your attention is called to Route Request Buttons that are installed on all new type Interlocking Home Signals where there is a choice of route in the midtown area. The route request button is to be operated by the motorman when the home signal is at danger and no call-on is displayed or when improper route is displayed.

To operate, the motorman will press the button for the desiredroute as indicated under each button; a light will then go on over the buttons to inform the motorman that his request has been registered in the tower.

If the towerman desires to give the motorman a route other than the one he selected, the towerman will cancel out the light over the route selection buttons. The motorman will then accept the route given.

If no route or call-on is given, the motorman will sound his whistle for the signal maintainer, secure his train, and call the desk trainmaster.

11. The official titles of the two classes of employee whose actions would MOST frequently   11.____
be affected by the contents of this notice are

    A. motorman and trainmaster
    B. signal maintainer and trainmaster
    C. towerman and motorman
    D. signal maintainer and towerman

12. A motorman should use a route request button when   12.____

    A. the signal indicates proceed on main line
    B. a call-on is displayed
    C. the signal indicates stop
    D. the signal indicates proceed on diverging route

13. The PROPER way to request a route is to   13.____

   A. press the button corresponding to the desired route
   B. press the button a number of times to correspond with the number of the route requested
   C. stop at the signal and blow four short blasts
   D. stop at the signal and telephone the tower

14. The motorman will know that his requested route has been registered in the tower if   14.____

   A. a light comes on over the route request buttons
   B. an acknowledging signal is sounded on the tower horn
   C. the light in the route request button goes dark
   D. the home signal continues to indicate stop

15. Under certain conditions, when stopped at such home signal, the motorman must signal   15.____
for a signal maintainer and call the desk trainmaster.
Such condition exists when, after standing awhile,

   A. the towerman continues to give the wrong route
   B. the towerman does not acknowledge the signal
   C. no route or call-on is given
   D. the light over the route request buttons is cancelled out

16. It is clear that route request buttons   16.____

   A. eliminate train delays due to signals at junctions
   B. keep the towerman alert
   C. force motormen and towermen to be more careful
   D. are a more accurate form of communication than the whistle.

Questions 17-22.

DIRECTIONS: Questions 17 through 22 are to be answered on the basis of the instructions for removal of paper given below. Read these instructions carefully before answering these questions.

GENERAL INSTRUCTIONS FOR REMOVAL OF PAPER

When a cleaner's work schedule calls for the bagging of paper, he will remove paper from the waste paper receptacles, bag it, and place the bags at the head end of the platform, where they will be picked up by the work train. He will fill bags with paper to a weight that can be carried without danger of personal injury, as porters are forbidden to drag bags of paper over the platform. Cleaners are responsible that all bags of paper are arranged so as to prevent their falling from the platform to tracks, and so as to not interfere with passenger traffic.

17. A GOOD reason for removing the paper from receptacles and placing it in bags is that   17.____
bags are more easily

   A. stored   B. weighed   C. handled   D. emptied

18. The *head end* of a local station platform is the end   18.____

    A. in the direction that trains are running
    B. nearest to which the trains stop
    C. where there is an underpass to the other side
    D. at which the change booth is located

19. The MOST likely reason for having the filled bags placed at the head end of the station   19.____
rather than at the other end is that

    A. a special storage space is provided there for them
    B. this end of the platform is farthest from the passengers
    C. most porters' closets are located near the head end
    D. the work train stops at this end to pick them up

20. Limiting the weight to which the bags can be filled is PROBABLY done to   20.____

    A. avoid having too many ripped or broken bags
    B. protect the porter against possible rupture
    C. make sure that all bags are filled fairly evenly
    D. insure that, when stored, the bags will not fall to the track

21. The MOST important reason for not allowing filled bags to be dragged over the platform   21.____
is that the bags

    A. could otherwise be loaded too heavily
    B. might leave streaks on the platform
    C. would wear out too quickly
    D. might spill paper on the platform

22. The instructions do NOT hold a porter responsible for a bag of paper which   22.____

    A. is torn due to dragging over a platform
    B. falls on a passenger because it was poorly stacked
    C. falls to the track without being pushed
    D. is ripped open by school children

Questions 23-25.

DIRECTIONS: Questions 23 through 25 are to be answered on the basis of the situation
                described below. Consider the facts given in this situation when answering
                these questions.

SITUATION

A new detergent that is to be added to water and the resulting mixture just wiped on any surface has been tested by the station department and appeared to be excellent. However, you notice, after inspecting a large number of stations that your porters have cleaned with this detergent, that the surfaces cleaned are not as clean as they formerly were when the old method was used.

23. The MAIN reason for the station department testing the new detergent in the first place was to make certain that   23.____

    A. it was very simple to use
    B. a little bit would go a long way
    C. there was no stronger detergent on the market
    D. it was superior to anything formerly used

24. The MAIN reason that such a poor cleaning job resulted was MOST likely due to the   24.____

    A. porters being lax on the job
    B. detergent not being as good as expected
    C. incorrect amount of water being mixed with the detergent
    D. fact that the surfaces cleaned needed to be scrubbed

25. The reason for inspecting a number of stations was to   25.____

    A. determine whether all porters did the same job
    B. insure that the result of the cleaning job was the same in each location
    C. be certain that the detergent was used in each station inspected
    D. see whether certain surfaces cleaned better than others

---

KEY (CORRECT ANSWERS)

1.	A		11.	C
2.	C		12.	C
3.	D		13.	A
4.	A		14.	A
5.	C		15.	C
6.	B		16.	D
7.	C		17.	C
8.	B		18.	A
9.	C		19.	D
10.	D		20.	B

21.	C
22.	D
23.	D
24.	B
25.	B
